ON THE EDGE

ON THE EDGE

Poems and
Essays from Russia

Andrei
Voznesensky

Translated by
Richard McKane

WEIDENFELD AND NICOLSON
LONDON

Published in Great Britain by
George Weidenfeld & Nicolson Limited
91 Clapham High Street
London SW4 7TA

ISBN 0 297 81061 8

Photoset by Deltatype Ltd, Ellesmere Port, Cheshire
Printed in Great Britain by
Butler and Tanner Ltd, Frome and London

✦ Contents ✦

✧ **Acknowledgements** ✧

'Troubadours and Burghers' and 'Applefall', translated with Michael Horovitz and Mara Amats, were first published in *New Departures*, and then in *Twentieth Century Russian Poetry*, edited and translated by Richard McKane (Kozmik Press, 1985, 1990). 'Up the Lighthouse' and parts of 'Ditch' were published in *Poetry of Perestroika* (Iron Press, 1991).

'The book is like a stroke of lightning. The translation is sharp and brilliant and very strong indeed. It deserves the highest praise and gratitude. The poems are wonderfully fresh and clear, and perfectly modern. They speak immediately and deeply to us.'

Peter Levi

The Lighthouse

ONE does not have to be a poet;
but it is not possible to stand
the screaming of the strip of light
squeezed in the door.

1976

The Candle Sculptor

I, the sculptor of candles, modelled you for over a year.
You are the best candle in the world for me.
I shake the matchbox, and strike up.
How grandly you flame
to the will of creator or executioner.

Was there ever a reason why a mother should burn her baby?
Work is the sin, not profit.
Did Turner burn his canvases?
How you burn!

You have two hours red wax in you.
Your briefer sisters gasp in rows
by others' bunks and posters,
how you burn!

How I sculpted my miracle child.
The springs were like incense. The roofs were dripping.
My mind was reeling. This was from the fumes.
This was from happiness of having you burn.

Round candles. Red spheres.
The white wick of unburnt heavenly bodies.
Eternal faith and the dark ages.
The black wick and the brief life of the body.

'I thank you and say farewell
to you for your short existence,
the flame, piercing without mercy,
along the backbone of the wick.

I thank you that your face and home
are lit up for a moment by me,
if you really said your name
this means that I shall burn in Your name.'

I, the sculptor of candles, will forget you,
hire a scooter and clear off
and stamp out stunned candles.
The tame crow has caught a cold and coughs.
Life is on the wane
like communication dishes,
and the cognac in the bottle goes down in time with the candle.

Black soot hangs on the eyelash
of the candle, unloved for a while.

First Love

We fell in love.
Your belly-button screwed-up
under your grandma's dressing gown
in this sort of country,
where vodka streamed down the knife
into tomato juice,
but never mixed with it.
We were in love.

We were in love. Squeeze the clods of freedom!
Under the moon outside the window sensed by dogs
but invisible to man,
Christ did not walk on the water,
but the tyrant of blood walked
on Caucasian boots with soft soles.
The tap spat blood under the out-house kitchen roof.
We walked, and did not know our guilt.
Love streamed into us, but never mixed with blood.
Forgive us that we were in love
in Stalin's times.

The Woman and the Wall

Hold the madwoman!
She ran amok and hit the wall,
with her full face and stomach of her uselessly beautiful body.
Her head cracked like an egg, her dress in rags foaming
against the wall.
She must be drunk.
Let me put you to bed, calm you, undress you
against the wall.

For the vulgarity of betrayal,
for the terrible price
of being beautiful and thoroughly modern,
for your body that tortures at night and at day,
about all the business-like beds,
about all the cramping impossibilities,
against the wall!

(After the impact her lower limbs
trembled for more than a minute like a Chopin trill.)

'Forgive this wall
that separated us inexorably.'
Forgive me, my darling man, that I did not kill you
to save you from captivity,
against the wall.

Forgive this scene.

The wall won. We are the shadows of the System.
Against the wall.
Blessèd be
the force of impact that breaks knees
and hurls one against the wall!

Suddenly you'll fly out, banging like a battering ram
through the wall–
leaving a hole outlining your body.

Clouds and night sirens fly through your body.
Blessèd be.

Up the Lighthouse in Lithuania

Like a maniac
I climb the old lighthouse.

I go out
onto the platform by the light.
Heat on my back. Midges sweat.

My shadow falls from the light
into double clouds of mist and swarming mosquitoes.

My head
lolls in the haze like that of a mutant.
Terrible haze all in my mind.

My bright plans are come from light,
my shaky life comes from the light.

My shadow lies heavy on my soul,
like granite flying from the light.

Light on the subconscious of the sea
and forest,
God and the devil,
on the look cast below.

Ah striped, burning truncheon of God,
point me out the way.

Light, in olden times,
you burned through the mist
saving the caravans of ships with your howl.
Electronic navigation is more convenient now.

But over waters
forests and seas
my shadow still moves from the light.

HOW lonely, to soar over
the dark, silent empire,
but I envy you, two-headed eagle,
for you can talk to yourself.

1978

BALLAD OF THE LAST DAYS
IN THE IPATYEV HOUSE

I broke the inner frame from the Ipatyev house,
out of the circle of the window,
thus preserving its life.
They liquidated the house without a sound.
God save the tsar!

This creaking wooden key,
the light from the window, the deceptive pattern,
they, who were shot, saw them point blank.
Fata Morgana, wipe the disc!
The boy is half-asleep . . .
'Children, what is the formula of the house of Romanov?'
'HCl'

God save the people of Russia that once was!
Acid rain has avenged us.
The window frame has impressed itself on the grey pupils
of the boy with his prophetic haemophilia.
You won't stop the bloodshed now.

I shall put the window frame
into my shack's window
and stretch out the cursed days
under its eye, widened by the torture
of the skies, with the impression of the window frame.
God save the country!

But what parting is poured
into the formula of hydrochloric acid?
And you wipe with your duster
the surrounding distance in the window frame
and the questioning look of the heights.

I will never dream of you.
I live you in reality.
I dream of all the rest.
And they're bad dreams.

You sleep on a cotton pillow.
You have caught the sun.
Your shaved armpit
breathes like a tea-strainer.

The Sophia Embankment.
The balcony door squeaks.
The honeyed metaphysics
of the lime trees that smell of you.

A Bar in New York

Part of my life emigrated.
It lived here. Put down roots.
It observes me now
with playful interest.

You shine like a diamond with facets
of eyes, nose – as in the dawn of a day.
But now you are a stone with sharp edges.
How did you come by this gift of the faceted frontier?

You were smashed into bits like an egg.
You tested the precipice on your flanks.
You run the Russian pub in New York
on heels of high desperation.

In this chic dark pit
I shall recognise – I'll come to you later–
your unbroken shining
like a small trove of diamonds.

I shall realise what no one knows,
what I hide and keep from myself.
The bouncer you gave a job
mocks me.

You ran vigorously down the humpbacked Moscow street,
you burst free into the world crash.
You shine. You are undamaged.
This is proof that you are a diamond.

Lithuanian Motifs

To J. Martsinkyavichus

Why do I never get tired of looking
at the Lithuanian sea at night?
It is the negative of a royal ermine cloak,
with white tails in black.

There are no fences here. The simple life.
Here a man carries a golden fish
from the corner shop,
like a rose wrapped in paper.

A Lithuanian girl, daughter of a quiet family,
throws herself out of the window
to escape the neighbourhood rapist,
carrying a knife, drunk.

Why do the words, concealed in our genes
come out in the steam room of the baths?
Why does Lithuania subconsciously
enter into all our prayers,
and why is 'Litva' [Lithuania]
hidden in our 'molitva' [prayer].

Forgive me, Justinas, the epics
that perished, the stagnant dead water,
and the secret protocols
of 1939.

Forgive me the Pyrrhic betrayal
of these people and forests,
it was the same leader that occupied us,
and he needed no protocol for the shootings.

Forgive me that our countries,
could not be returned.
Justinas, you see things clearer than us.
But to whom can I ask these questions?

CURFEW TIME

At curfew time –
muffle the oars.
The wave flames like a threatening razor.
The patrols stand
at the borders of the soul.

The shops are empty
in the curfew hour.
Only the Kalashnikov's magazine is full of goods.
The masses' conscience
is automaticised.
The Maxim machine guns
hurtle in the back of Zhiguli cars.

A peasant woman screams
at the burial:
'I nursed two babies at my two breasts.
Boys of two bloods.
I gave them my nipples
not cartridges.'

The night is deep and dull. History's mole is dark.
'Stop the bloodshed!
Stop the bloodshed!'
Paul, grown hoarse, appeals with her:
'He's neither a Hellene nor a Jew . . .'

From eleven at night to six in the morning –
in Our Fathers and the Muslim hours of prayer,
in curfew time –
our blood creeps into hiding
like a viper.
Anything could happen.

Where are you lying awake now,
my almond eyes?
Your brown skin divides your stomach in half.
Who are your ancestors? Scythians?
Georgians? Abkhazians?
Let the year of the curfew
enter into you.

We look at ourselves
and see such chaos.
Your blood carries on a thousand-year-old feud with your soul.
Two crowds came together
with rifles by the river.
The centifugal country
whirled round.

And a peasant woman in black,
screams like a prophet rock. 'Stop the bloodshed!
Stop the bloodshed!'

The black ribbon flags
are like blindfolds.
Lord forgive us who have been blinded.
The Third Guard
asks for your documents.
It's curfew time
according to TASS.

A. Men

Who raised the axe against the priest?
Who followed him in the cold of the early morning?
How can we find forgiveness in the heart
for what we are doing now?
The man who raised the axe against the priest
damned himself. Amen.

Is my country so desperately
sick in its degradation
that it's gone beyond sacrilege
to axerilege?

He was a beautiful man. He spent all his time
softening hearts in these dark times.
The murdered man had knocked at his own front door.
His wife did not recognize him.

The axe took the dispute
right to the vertebrae of his neck.
A country that murders priests
writes its own death sentence.

He had been a friend of Tarkovsky –
the unprotected aorta loves the heart.
They went to school 554
together.

And I went to school with you.
On behalf of our school 554,
I light this candle in mourning for you
at your Requiem.

A parish in the heart of Russia.
The Afghan 'vets! The blue of onion domes.
A girl intones with a sigh
after the liturgy: 'A. Men . . . Amen . . .'

And tipping the bloody scales
in the sky over our dawn way,
foretold by Dostoyevsky
with cosmic authenticity
the axe flies like a sputnik.

NEW VILLAGE
CHURCH OF THE PURIFICATION
10/IX/90

CHAGALL'S CORNFLOWERS

Your face is silver as a halebard.
Your gestures are light.
There are dried cornflowers in a jar
in your rough hotel.

My dear, these are your real loves.
You were wounded by them and loved by them since Vitebsk,
those little tubes of wild weed
with devilishly expressed blue.

An orphan flower from the burdock family,
but its blue knows no rival.
The enigma of Chagall, Marc Chagall,
the loudspeaker of the Savelovo train station.

This all grew out of the Russian saints Boris and Gleb,
in the laughter of New Economic Policy and Caucasian
                              meat pasties.
Corn in the fields, and a little sky.
Man lives by heaven alone.

The blue notches of the stained-glass windows,
with their pure Gothic tension upwards.
The field is loved, but the sky is beloved.
Man lives by heaven alone.

Cows and water-sprites soar in the sky,
open your umbrella as you go onto the street.
Homelands are different, but the sky is the same.
Man lives by heaven alone.

How did the cornflower seed get
to the Champs Élysées, the Elysian fields?
How did you weave your wreath on the brow
of the Grand Opera, the Grand Opera?

There is no sky in the age of mass consumerism.
The artist's lot is worse than the cripple's.
It's ridiculous to give them silver coins.
Man lives by heaven alone.

Your canvases escaped
the Fascist madness and the bigots.
The forbidden sky was rolled into a tube
but man lives by heaven alone.

Russia, who kissed your fields
till they brought forth cornflowers?
Your wild plants are the most beautiful in the world,
why don't you export them?

You come off the train to such a welcome!
The fields tremble.
The field is studded with cornflowers,
the further you go, the farther it stretches.

If you get out by evening, the field is full
of Uglich eyes, and you feel sick.
Oh, Marc Zakharovych, Marc Zakharovych,
there are cornflowers everywhere.

Let not Jehovah or Jesus,
but you, Marc Zakharovych Chagall, paint
the insuperably blue covenant:
'Man lives by heaven alone.'

Look Back Into the Future

We fly forwards
and look back.
What heaven it was!
What hell it was!
People of my country,
look back into the future.

DEAR writer colleagues!
How happy I am,
that in our common prosperity
I alone am sworn at.

As the black sheep of the family,
I do not live my life in vain –
I highlight the perfection
of my impeccable colleagues.

VIDEOPOEM

'What co-operative
shall we start?'
is all the rage in this country.

My partner-in-crime
started a co-op to sell videomoney.

5 golden fish
can buy a bucket of videoroubles.
Videoathletes. Videovictories.
Videodinners for videomoney.
Videosubscriptions. Videoretirements.

Videoworries. Videofreedom.
On videosaturdays I creep in
from videowork to my videofamily.
Videocows give us milk to drink.
Videoapplause. Videolives.

A physically dead tyrant rules within us.
We are the metaphysical videoshowpeople.

Videopacified, videopeople,
videouniformed into videopolice.
Videoforecasts. Videolargescale,
and videotears at funerals

Who thought up this co-operative?
How can one deprogram it?
Who wants huge slogans on walls:
'Socialism is the videofication of the whole country!'

Assembly of bells. Disassembly of rockets.
The snowy forest races like an abstract Classical sculptor.
Where are you racing to, Russia. Answer!
The answer is reality, not video.

Forest Ballad

I take you into my safekeeping
from the confines of Moscow vanity.
You are like a copse that has been cut down.
You screamed to me: 'Protect me!'

We turn friends away.
Let us put coals on the homely stove,
and pour on a glass of forest moonshine vodka,
so that the flames should turn blue.

In these hastening, fiery coals,
in a hoarse word that bursts out,
there's a sense of a crime,
that once would have been called a sin.

It was freedom that I did not have enough of.
It's a sin that we are a third serfs.
We split so much dead wood:
it's good that it's burning now in the sad stove.

There is no sense of a romance here:
this is how it is with fire and rain –
you come to bed, slightly pale,
having washed the make-up off your face.

The telephone, so connected with your former life,
like a white skull with a snake,
will stir and ring in vain,
in the flat that you have forsaken.

In this log hunting cabin,
as in a country sanctuary,
we are wedded to wild freedom;
and I bet you have gypsy blood in you.

I take you into my safekeeping,
in the face of the city and before all peoples.
Take me into your safekeeping,
with the angel of freedom and suffering as your witness.

APPLEFALL

I visited the artist after death
accompanied by a local she-devil.
His rooms were empty as frames without pictures;
but the sound of Tchaikovsky came from one of them.

I walked through the deserted halls
with my tall Afro-haired guest;
it was like holding onto a black balloon.

Behind a door, in an armchair,
sat a thought in the form of a woman
surrounded by forty portraits.
The thought hit me – like a creative impulse –
signalling: don't interrupt.

What a strain to be an artist's model!
Three-legged easels laboured over her.
I sensed loneliness
in their swirling, ever changing structures –

here a nail, there three eyes, a captured bayonet –
how he must have loved her then!
No fulfilment
for the creative impulse.

Above the radiator Tchaikovsky
revolved under Gennady Rozhdestvensky's
baton. My Afro-balloon pleaded
to be loosed to the winds. A thunderstorm
crashed in the sky. Clouds exuded the scent
of apple sacks.

Everyone was feeling it now –
as though the impulse preceding creation
the passion preceding creation,
the sorrow preceding creation
rocked the buildings and the trees!

Apples fell. The strings
and boughs were weeping:
so many apples, you could shovel them up!
On my knees I gathered them,
these fallen apples of the applefall.
I threw off my shirt: like cold fists
they bastinadoed my naked shoulderblades.
I guffawed under the applefall;
there was no apple tree –
just apples falling.
I tied the sleeves of my chastened shirt
and stuffed it full of fruit like a basket.
How heavy it weighed, and trembling, redolent –
I gasped –
a woman was sat there in a man's shirt . . .

I had created you from fallen apples –
out of dust – my marvellous one, my waif!
Under your sideways-slanting eye was stuck
a birthmark like a tiny dark grain.
I'd played co-author to creation.
That's how we make snowmen in the yard
from snow-apples, on our knees –
that's how we make our lovers.
I introduced you as a guest to the lady of the house.
You handed your Eve's apples out to all the guests
and earthed them with your black jive-talk.

Who would have guessed that you, smiling there
in a short little mini-dress
would forget yourself, fall in love, throw off your shirt
and roll on the ground like balls of quicksilver . . .

Above the bus stop a cloud
smelled of winter apple sacks.
The black balloon flew off. Wind swept over the world.
Farewell spontaneous creation!

Had you spent the night in the creator's dacha
cold and alone, on prickly sackcloth?

These words came to you:
'Thank you for your giving. Much thanks, creator
that I was able to be part of you,
part of the sea and dry land, of Tsvetayeva's garden.
Thanks for granting me all this:
that I haven't lived my life like a mouse in a hole,
that I haven't double-dealt with you, Time,
even when you gave me two fingers –
and thanks for these frenzied blows,
for my putting paper to pen, even,
and for this poem;
and though you'll snuff it tomorrow
I thank you for giving me
the short sweet apples of her knees,
for the geniality of your models,
the unnameable uniqueness of your ideas . . .'

And, already dreaming, repeated:
'I worship you for your gifts.'

Night gates opened into the world.
You went away. Dogs howled.
It's no good visiting the artist when he's dead –
do it while you're still alive.

TRANSLATED WITH MICHAEL HOROVITZ AND MARA AMATS

WHEN one day I die,
do not torment the grass or mushrooms,
understand me in my last joke,
and smile.

When you're going home at night with the shopping,
that's when I'll run ahead
and light the long mercury tubes
on their black trunks.

Recognize me in the waste land,
in my habitual gestures . . .
And if you live in a house in town –
I'll call the lift for you.

From the Lives of
O's and X's

The Way of the Cross

+   +   +

Two sticks went flying. One to the North,
the other to the West. Their shadows crossed,
and formed a cross.
'Sticks, don't fly apart, please,
or I'll disappear.'
'Sorry, little cross, it's time for us to go.'

+   +   +

The cross was going down the road
It saw a crowd of little crosses on a branch.
'Are you a regional assembly of crosses?'
'No, we are the lilac.'
The cross got sad, and threw up its arms.
It went on.

+   +   +

It went on and saw some black crosses on top of each other
like a gymnastic display.
'Hi, cult of the physical! Peace, peace, peace!! Can I
stand on you for a minute?'
'Of course! We are the prison bars. Come and join us,
It just threw up its arms.
'I am sorry, I am in a hurry.'
We'll tell you later where he was off to.

+   +   +

Man came from the monkey. But where did crosses come from?
From man. If you plant a dead person in the earth
(and water them) a cross will grow.
But many think that their origin is not of this world

31

It was a cross that first discovered America. It was up on the mast.

+   +   +

They say that it was a cross that dropped the bomb on Hiroshima.

+   +   +

The cross was afraid of AIDS. It went into the chemist and bought a condom.
'Which of my four members do I put it on?'

+   +   +

When the crosses were choosing a minister of fisheries, he stood on the stage and opened his arms and said: 'We'll catch fish this big.'

+   +   +

A woman came to get laid with a cross.
'Little cross, can I hang my blouse on you? But don't wriggle or you'll tear it.'
She took her blouse off. Lay down. Waited. Went to sleep.
The cross hung on till morning, not daring to move.

+   +   +

When the crosses went on strike, all the exercise books in squares became lines. What's more. Everyone's clothes fell apart, and people on the street were suddenly naked. One woman was left standing in a red leather skirt, and she regretted that bitterly.

+   +   +

The cross became a deputy of the Soviet Parliament

On its own at the same time a cross can;
shake hands with four voters,
or
pick up four telephones
or pick up two receivers and shake two hands
or
at a reception hold, whisky, champagne, a sausage and a salami sandwich,
or
order the people forward in four directions
at the same time.

+   +   +

A cross came to get an exit visa.
'Are you going to Israel?'
'No I want to reunite my family'
'Are you husband or wife?'
'No I am reunitement itself. I am the "plus" sign. For instance
John + Darya, Alexey + Peggy.'
'It's all right for them, but you're not allowed.'
The cross burst into tears. 'Why did I queue for so long?'
He just threw up his hands.

+   +   +

The cross was drafted into the army. He was very good at
marching in ceremonies. 'By the left . . . Quick Maaarch!' The
cross was sent to the Kremlin academy.

+   +   +

When the crosses were persecuted, the cross brought a stick. It
pretended to be a five-pointed star.

+   +   +

One day the cross was driving down Gorky Street in a white
Volga. It looked up at a nude statue on the roof, and was distracted.
The cross turned red. There was an accident. This is why
ambulances have red crosses.

+   +   +

The cross got so drunk, that it had to be carried home.
'What do you think you are doing, multiplication?'

+   +   +

Noughts are the enemies of crosses, at least that's what the cross
was told by its grandmother. The cross did not listen and got
married to the nought and they became a sniper's sight.

+   +   +

Crosses did not know how to read or write, but they loved to sign
orders. It is well-known that three novels and seven memoirs have
been signed with crosses.

+ + +

Koestler came to Russia, and was not confiscated at the border.

'I want to go to Suzdal.'

'You're welcome. Presumably you want to see a political camp?'

'No, I translated the poem "I live in the Russia of snows and saints." '

He was all rosy. His wife was young.

He translated 'First Snow'. Millions of crystalline crosses froze on the windows of the telephone box.

+ + +

When the noughts beat the crosses, they put the prisoners in pairs, back to back, in two ranks. Thus the railway was born. Noughts rode down it.

Then the crosses beat the noughts. They walked round the platform and rode on the noughts, looking out of windows of the coaches. They left the railways to themselves.

+ + +

'Lie on your belly and relax, lift your legs to your shoulders. They'll plant a Christmas tree in you. Do not move in case the crosses fall off like needles.'

+ + +

Crosses are faithful in love. The cross raised his love in its arms. He did not know where to put her – nothing was good enough for her. And so they died in each others' arms.

The cross is the memorial of eternal love.

Eyelash, Awake!

+   +   +

The cross was flying in the sky, and an eyelash was coming to meet him.
'Let's live together.'
'But stop jerking your leg, and winking at people in the street.'

+   +   +

How they flew! Often she trembled and her eyes were wet but it was with tears of happiness.
Twice the melody of The Godfather Cross came into their dreams.

+   +   +

She told him her whole life story. How she delivered letters after school. How she collapsed and fell and the sign of a tiny cross was made over her and she was put in someone's bosom.
'To the letters, the letters' and to the call blue envelopes flew to be stuck down crossways.
He was jealous, but they grew stronger together.

+   +   +

He woke one day and the eyelash was not there. Perhaps she was in the bathroom?
Shedding abundant tears. He waited, she was nowhere.
The wound of parting hurt on the left side.

+   +   +

Cranes, have you seen my eyelash? Cat on the roof have you seen my eyelash? Broom have you seen my eyelash.
The Godfather Cross theme is heard in the distance
The cross went travelling round the country.

+   +   +

He went through the towns that bustled with crosses, like the knitted socks or the anthills, he went by mended villages, over the fields, the

35

sewn up cornflower crosses, through the elegant crowds on the pavements who wore Adidas shawls.

He walked and threw up his arms.

'Haven'tyouseenmyeyelash?'

But no one knew about the eyelash.

+ + +

The cross went to the sculptor Ernst Neizvestny. The sculptor tore his chest in two, shoved in a nought and twisted his legs with pliers – and hung him on the wall in the Vatican.

Your most holiness, excuse me but have you not seen my eyelash?

+ + +

The cross flew through the living room window. He burst into song and hit the highest note. He sang of the eyelash. People rushed up to him and clapped their hands. Clap, clap! 'You're a malarial mosquito!'

'Applause is dangerous' he decided and flew on further.

+ + +

The cross went out on the roof like a sleepwalker. There were many crosses up there. He walked on balancing with his arms. A blue cat who was in love came towards him.

'Little cross, I'm depending on you. Now she loves me now she doesn't, she spits at me then kisses me.'

The cat tore off his arms and legs and there was just a dot left.

'Don't worry, you'll grow again, and you did help a friend.'

+ + +

The cross went to Rostropovich.

'Maestro, please tell me why all my life I scratch my bow across my belly, but no music emerges?'

'Did you try putting rosin on yourself?'

'I'm sorry but, by the way, haven'tyouseenmyeyelash?'

+ + +

Two black government *Volgas* sat on an oak. Their doors slammed, they crowed:

'Cross, come to us and go in the centre of the steering wheel.'

'Oh yes, but you'll break my fourth leg. You need three spokes to go in a steering wheel. Excuse me, haven'tyouseenmyeyelash?'

'Cr! Cr! Go down the road to the crossroads and turn right, or rather left, by the traffic police post.'
Then they honked their hooter that played the Godfather Cross theme.

+   +   +

When he felt particularly sad, he stood at the crossroads and played his flute. A weak echo from the Godfather Cross theme answered him.

+   +   +

Joyce called women flutes with three holes. The cross didn't count. He was into the music.

+   +   +

They caught the cross. They tied his hands over his head. They shackled his wrists and ankles. They threw him on the road. He tried to free himself. He puffed out his elbows and knees in coils on out into infinity. Infinity is a shackled cross.

+   +   +

They broke the arms and legs of the cross in the cooler. They bent them back.
'We'll show you, you fascist.'
'What sort of fascist was he? He was just a broken cross.'

+   +   +

After that the cross started stammering. He stammered all the time. 'I am a cr-cr-cross', he said introducing himself.

+   +   +

At the bottom of the highroad near Moscow there was anti-tank barbed wire.
'The group sex of crosses'.

+   +   +

He walked for a long time and just threw up his hands.

+   +   +

The godfather cross reclined at the centre of the Universe, on a red Swiss army knife. Four blades of privileged steel were hidden beneath him, scissors, wings, a file, a bottle opener, a magnifying glass and eyelash tweezers.

In case of emergency the godfather cross surreptitiously got out a screwdriver (the one with the cross at the end) for the tape recorder: the lynch-pin of reproduction.
The Godfather Cross theme welled up.

If you cut up that sort of a screwdriver into tiny bits, you get wonderful steel crosses. They make very good food. They are pesticide free. They remain in the human organism for 170 years without rusting. And they give off signals.

The godfather cross lay back, examining an eyelash under a magnifying glass, which was dancing before him on a crystal ball, or rather a round teardrop.

'Haven'tyouseenmyeyelash? Give me back my eyelash!'
'What's this? A peasant cross? What, a surprise? We've decrossified the country long ago. Send it to chop wood.'

The privileged ones grabbed. The last thing he saw was the eyelash sliding and falling off the teardrop. The tweezers picked her up.

There were millions of crosses sawing down trees with him. The frosts got fiercer. They turned into crystals. Twenty years went by. The cross left twenty notches on the pole.

Twice he saw the red knife, bristling with blades, crossing the blue sky.

The Godfather Cross theme welled up.

He was released. He set off across the country, and threw up his arms.

The godfather cross reclined on the red knife. The eyelash was dancing before him, surrounded by eighteen dancing daughters. Oh f. . . ! The godfather cross raised the magnifying glass over the stranger. The cross felt his arms growing into a giant's, like the beams of a searchlight, or the girders of a construction crane. His arms were gigantic!

The cross hit the red knife with a bang. The magnifying glass shattered. Our hero became microscopic again.

'Bastard! I'll crush you myself. Who do you think you are crossing the red system.'

+   +   +

A duel! A duel! The knives and scissors flashed. The Godfather Cross theme roared out at 100 decibels. All the blows of the cross were deflected by the red armour. Two extremities of the cross were cut off. The godfather cross prepared for the *coup de grâce*. He put the cross up against the wooden wall, took a run, and swinging the knife over his head, drove the big blade through the unfortunate cross pinning him to the wall.

'Finale of the cross?' Pinned to the wall in the *coup de grâce*! But then a streak of blue lighting flashed.

The cat! You protected your comrade, and lost half of a paw. But you deflected the knife blow a couple of millimetres. The cross is saved! The knife went up to the hilt into the wall and stuck there. My eyelash, are you winking at me? I get it. The cross gathered all his strength and jumped onto the godfather cross, and sank a screw into him and screwed him up.

The godfather cross disintegrated.

+   +   +

'Hurrah! We were always for glasnost and pluralism. The tyrant is dead! Hail to the new godfather cross.'

'No, my friends, I am only a tiny cross. Come, cat, lean on me.'
'We're not quits yet.' The cat said: 'I still owe you three paws.'
'I only know how to play the flute. Let me go away for a minute and calm down. I am not a ratcatcher, I'm a cross. I'll play for you, then be on my way.'
'My love, I was a captive, all my life I loved only you. I never flew in the sky like that with anyone else, growing into the five fingered lilac.'

'I love you too. All I wanted was for you to be happy. I never flew in the sky like that with anyone else, growing into the five fingered flower.'

He started playing his flute. When the sound finished they looked round, wiping their tears and began to search for the cross.
It was nowhere to be seen.

+   +   +   .

They say he was spotted in Voronezh. Sometimes you can hear his flute on the radio.

+   +   +

When the cross died he was buried.

'What if we buried him the wrong way up?'

They dug him up and turned him upside down and buried him.

'What if we buried him the wrong way up?'

They dug him up and turned him upside down and buried him.

'What if we buried him the wrong way up?'

They dug him up and turned him upside down and buried him.

'Let it be!'

THE GENEALOGY OF CROSSES

The microscope revealed a world of miracles.
The slide revealed that the world consists of crosses.

+   +   +

If all the crosses joined hands and made a chain, the column would stretch from Vilnius to Tallinn.

+   +   +

Women begin the beginning. ♀ – is not Venus's mirror. It is the kiss of a cross and a nought, or Charlie Chaplin, or the 0 of Catherine the Great, as the poet remarked.

+   +   +

Crosses love to play at throwing sticks. It's very nice when the arms and legs fly apart. Their favourite reading matter is crosswords.

+   +   +

There are flying crosses with six extremities – including two wings. The anti-Semites created standards for crosses. If the cross is shorter than the standard, it is a Zionist.

+   +   +

Crosses are allowed to appear on TV. But there is a censor assigned to count the number of rays in the stars on the screen, in case there are any Stars of David.

+   +   +

When the noughts surrounded the crosses, the two surviving ones stood back to back with their sub-machine guns at the ready.

+   +   +

Are you a cross that goes from right to left or left to right? A Polish cross or a Russian one? If the answer is yes, we'll shoot you.

+   +   +

The white crosses scored a goal. They jumped on each other for joy, all in a heap, embracing and waving their arms about.
They flew into the skies with joy.
Snowflakes fell.

+   +   +

When Stalin swore his oath of allegiance to Lenin, the words on his moustache froze like white crosses.

+   +   +

We are floundering in the sand dunes.
'Something's tugging at my back.'
'It must be the pull of latitude and longitude.'

+   +   +

Three crosses above and one below. Don Quixote and the windmills.
Don Quixote beat the windmill. He built the Atomic Power Station.
The crosses were added on.

+   +   +

A ball met the crosses. It ate them. It ate so many that they spilled out of his belly. They called it a gooseberry.

+   +   +

They say that Kerensky dressed up as a nurse. He drew a red cross on his forehead. He ran away. Alexander F. told me this was not true.
They say that in fact he dressed up as a sailor, and put on a sailor's cap, and ran away. This is also not true. Read Berberova.

+   +   +

Cross, where is the exit?
Over there!

+   +   +

The cross rises from the chair, showing you that the audience is over.

+   +   +

Champion X swam the Styx.
Mister X, sir?

+   +   +

This isn't poetry or prose, it's craziness.
The cross just threw up its hands.

A Passion for XXL

The cross got divorced. He had three daughters and a son from the nought's sister.

The elder one was an umbrella. She was the spit image (especially in profile) in her upper half of a half nought, and in her lower half of a half cross.

When she grew up, she went to work in a café in town, and in the summer moved onto the beach. After midnight she let down her short skirt, and in the morning she opened it up for her clients.

The younger one worked there as an ice-cream bowl, that could contain three noughts. The third worked as a paperweight.

The boy went out onto the boulevard with a sharpened spoke. When he poked the passers-by, they became crosses.

He worked in space as a compass. (His weightlessness was useful. It didn't matter where his head hung.) But where is north and where is south in space? They laid the cross off.

He became a pole vaulter.

When he worked as a driller, he became so distracted that he drilled into the centre of gravity. He caught onto the centre and dragged it up to the surface like the nerve of a tooth.

The earth itself was falling apart. The deserted equator was riding roughshod over the stones.

The nought was rolling with laughter.

The centre of gravity was returned to place, but not quite to the right place. The earthquakes continued. They paid off the cross and transferred him to some other work.

When the Big Cross was driven in the black Volga limousine he couldn't fit in, and one of his ends stuck out of the roof like an antenna.

When they took away his limousine he started taking the trolleybus, and one of his ends stuck out of the roof and bent back to touch the wires.

He did a night job, as a red light on an airstrip. All the planes of the world made their descent towards him.

When the cross was making TV programmes, he divided the screen into four quadrants. Four programmes could be seen on the screen at once.
On his left shoulder the Party Assembly was on the platform; on his right shoulder Miss Central Zone was being elected; under his left shoulder the workers were demanding that the Mausoleum and State Dachas be handed over to the party of sexual minorities; and under his right armpit a deputee rushed up to the microphone with the idiotic face of a rock star.

He suddenly had the feeling that his left shoulder had collapsed under a burning weight. Isolda, the new Miss Central Zone, went up onto the pedestal. All the pants burst like balloons.
Her arse wouldn't fit in the Guiness Book of Records. The cross found it very hard to hold her up on his shoulder.

The ceiling of the Assembly tilted up like a deck. The party of sexual minorities was in a huddle, and the deputee was leading a rock group in a number.
Isolda squeezed herself into a hoola-hoop and got stuck.

'Mademoiselle Isolda, what have you been reading this last year.' 'I have read the T shirts of 142 admirers. I liked most the text on my boyfriend Seryozha's T shirt. I do like to read, but reading in bed isn't good for one . . .'

In the morning the cross woke up with a fever. All four thermometers which were shoved into him showed his temperature as forty.

+   +   +

They hospitalised him. They wrapped him in a sheet and carried him on a stretcher. He pierced the sheet, and his red extremities stuck out. 'You're like a cemetery in the snow,'
The nought said and rolled on past.

He woke up on the examination table. The woman doctor was making her diagnosis:
'A strained shoulder.'
'Radiation sickness' said another woman doctor.
'All four rays are inflamed.'
'Perhaps he's in love,' said the professor.
'With Isolda,' the nurse said,
'Everyone saw them yesterday.'

'No,' Isolda said.

+   +   +

One Sunday he lifted Isolda in the meadow and her weight drove him into the ground and up to the cross beam.

+   +   +

He met her in the lift. He turned pale, tore himself out of himself and lifted her like a four-petalled lily.
'No,' Isolda said whiningly.

+   +   +

Another time he went even whiter. He rolled himself up and gave himself to her as a pressed handkerchief.
Isolda blew her nose on him.

+   +   +

'What woman would like such a thin person? Look at yourself in the mirror.' said the nought.
He bought some weights. He took up body building. Within a month his biceps were bulging and he was like the ace of clubs.
'No,' said Isolda.

+   +   +

'I'll drown myself,' he thought and jumped off a bridge. A chain of bubbles ran after him. He hung on to the silver chain.

'It takes half an hour to swim round the whole of Isolda doing breast stroke.' the nought said.

+ + +

'Women love servicemen,' the nought said.
The cross joined the army. But he just couldn't carry out the order to stand to attention.
'No,' Isolda said after three years.

+ + +

'It's she who's ill,' the nought said. How couldn't he realise it? She was always catching cold without her knickers. It was draughty down there. He knew her size: 'XXL, Extra-Extra-Large.'
He scoured the country. But none of the stores had that size.
The nought said: 'Perhaps they have XXL in America.'

THE CROSS IN AMERICA

The cross was going to fly over to America.
Aeroflot had no tickets available for five years. Skyjackers were on
stand-by for six months.

THEN HE FAXED HIMSELF OVER

. . . Reader, have you ever been transferred by Fax, feeling that a
certain seraphic power has split you into dots – but what if it can't
group you together again, forgets the code, or muddles it up with
others? Have you ever been translated like lightning into another
dimension, frozen with horror at the speed of thought and crazed
commas. Once Russia was a troika, hurtling into nowhere, but
America, are you not a wild Fax, gone out of control, rushing and
buzzing, while the bridges fly beneath you?

He came to on the 109th floor. Pale blue oval noughts in crimson
frames were examining him.
'Dear fox Fax, I'll Tipp-ex your misprint.'
A purple-lacquered nail-tip flicks the cross off the page and out of the
window, like a tiny insect.
The office manager continued her telephone conversation:
'Hello. Yes it's Audrey. Everything is fine. It's just that our naughty
nought's got pregnant again. Yes, long distance. We suspect a cross
from Hong Kong.'

The burning perpendiculars of avenues and streets flashed beneath
him.
O, New, York, New York – world capital of crosses!

He landed on all fours like a kitten.
'Tell me, how do I get to Bloomingdale's?'
'5/47 – and then right on to 3/59 . . .' It's not so much a city, more a crossword puzzle. A Bobby Fisher dream gone mad.
New Yorkers are children of rectangles and think in chess knight's moves.

Thousands of crosses were jogging in Central Park in their T-shirts and shorts, white, black, yellow and blue. There were noughts among them too. Children's smiles flashed, showing silver braces on their teeth.
Just a few pairs of noughts were topless, and a very few bottomless.

The cross took his clothes off and joined the file.
'Nudists are in fashion now,' the blue glasses said as they passed him, and their wearer left cross-like bird tracks on the track.
'So she's a bird as well,' the cross thought.

In the gleaming shop window of Bloomingdale's there were 1,000 red Swiss army penknives.
We used to think our godfather cross knife was the only one.
They were astir with blades, magnifying glasses and antennae. One of them had a brush sticking out for cleaning a pipe or a lavatory pan. It was like a red Buckingham Palace guardsman in a bearskin.

In the next shop window there were sparkling diamonds.
They had crossed rays instead of facets.
They pleaded: 'Free us, smash the window!'

But knickers in XXL were nowhere to be found.

When he was going round the first floor of a supermarket he grabbed a sausage off the floor and ate it, with the wrapping on it. No one noticed. But when he came to the check-out, the shoplifted sausage let out a howl inside him.

With his stomach howling he ran down Lexington Avenue, and the howls of the noughts of police cars and motorcycles were in hot pursuit.

ATTENTION ALL CARS AND PERSONNEL! An unidentified cross is proceeding down Lexington Avenue. Distinguishing features: he only has four fingers. Believed to be a stranger in town.

On the corner of 42nd street he put into action an old Russian thieves' trick. 'Split the bloody hell out! Make for the Rock Centre roof,' he said, in incomprehensible Russian slang. One of his legs flew north, the others split and headed off in different directions.
Meanwhile the sausage descended into the lower leg.

The police truncheons and noughts of handcuffs chased after the black leg-sticks like shadows.

They united again on the roof of the Rockefeller Centre. Three had come up in the lifts, and waited for the fourth, who climbed up the fire escape, howling the while. When they were reunited, the cross looked round in all four directions.

But why were the whole crowd's eyes and all the cameras trained on the roof? And why was there a rope, attached to the roof, stretching to the Empire State Building? Obviously some tightrope walker or other was preparing for a Guinness Book of Records attempt.

But our cross got there first. His howls were apocalyptical as he made his way, balancing himself with his arms over the yawning chasm; as he made his way above the rectangles of New York that were all holding their breath, walking with the stately paces of a guardsman or a queen.

He's made it to the Empire State Building, and applause roars out. The cross held out his arms in victory. That was when they put the handcuffs on him.

'Now you're for the electric chair.'
They clipped on the plus electrode to the cross. Since he was a plus, there was no effect.
They put on the minus: he made an immediate connection. A joyful energy flowed through him.
'Please increase the current!' he begged the operators, his eyes wincing with pleasure.
   They threw him out.

They didn't give him anywhere to stay. The Soviet homeless are used to this in a different way. He folded himself up into a dash, like a folded umbrella, and slept on a bench.

He counted four little stars above him. 'Tonight I'm sleeping in a four star hotel,' he thought to himself and went to sleep sweetly.

He dreamed of fields of clover, where crosses flew from flower to flower, and pricked their proboscises deep in them, and stuck out with their antennae vibrating happily.

Little bundles of memory hung in the autumn air, like cobwebs. Who wove them. What do they mean?

He looked at the sky a lot. The communications of the rains streamed from a Fax cloud. The communications of steam rose into the sky from Fax lawns.

He dreamed of his mother, when he was a seven-year-old child. She was sleeping. He drew a cross on her left buttock, and began to draw one on her right. But he had just drawn the (−), when there was a short circuit. He never saw his mother again.

+   +   +
+

Ah, a forty-eight-star hotel . . .

+   +   +
+

It started getting cold. From the Fax in the skies a communication of white Zhivago crosses flew down to earth. 'The snowstorm drew circles and crosses on the window pane.'

+   +   +
+

He noticed that the American doors have cross-shaped key holes. So he began to get into empty flats.

+   +   +
+

In one bedroom there were some glasses with red frames on a stool. There was a Macintosh Fax rustling in the corner. There were some dry bird tracks leading to the bathroom. So this is where you live.

+   +   +
+

He waited. The letters and numbers were being printed on the T shirts. Where can one Fax oneself to, while the lady is in the bathroom?
There was a set of telephone books on the side.

+   +   +
+

He opened one of the telephone books at random. There was a telephone number listed for some Felix Yusupov. He dialled.
He came to in Rasputin's beard. The monk scratched himself. He caught the cross. 'I'll squash you with my nail!' A shot rang out. His fingers let go.

+   +   +
+

The cross panicked and telephoned again. He couldn't remember what number he'd dialled.

A man with a moustache was sitting in a study. HE FINISHED SMOKING HIS PIPE AND KNOCKED THE CROSS OUT WITH THE ASH. 'YOU DON'T EXIST IN FACT . . .'
'Not in fact, but I do in Fax . . .

+   +
+

He was back in the room with the red glasses. Time Magazine of the year 2014 was lying on the stool.
THE WOMAN SAID: 'ARE YOU GOING TO GIVE ME A PRESENT FROM THAT XXth CENTURY OF YOURS? THERE HAVE BEEN CASES OF AIDS BEING TRANS- MITTED BY FAX . . .

+   +
+

'Who's stretched my knickers? How dare you!' Audrey flew out of the bath. 'Oh, it's you again, Fax-fox! I thought so. Don't look at my legs. Imagine I'm behind a screen. Do you think that because I've got no dressing gown, I'm quite defenceless?' She held up at shoulder level the cord from her dressing gown, and looked out as though from behind a screen. Wipe the floor round me. Not so quick. Her oval nought turned round with surprise.
'Oh! Oh, no! ± − . . . O! +oo++oh! − O darling O+++! How quick you are, oh, you've got four x's . . . I searched for you on all the Faxes. But there wasn't anyone like you. Let's go into the bathroom. Give me all four again. More, more! That's great! The fourth is the best!

+   +
+

'You're a real cross. While we were making love, a thousand crosses thrust out of your cheeks and chin. Whole squadrons of raw recruits, and they were all prickly.'
'Let's shave them into nought.'

+   +
+

'What's that circle on your left elbow?' In our country the doctors mark the children with a minus. Then this minus flares up into a nought: and you have it for life.

+   +
+

There was a photo of a nought on the wall. Is that your husband? No, it's my mother. She hatched us all. 'Ah, you're my little bird.'

+   +   +
+

'I read that Russians talk about State Electrification, while having sex. Tell me about SE.'

+   +   +
+

He moved in with her. He helped round the house. He was a useful four-bladed meat mincer. When she wasn't there, he used to travel by Fax. The Macintosh suited him well.

+   +   +
+

WHAT JOY: TO ENTER THE SOFTWARE OF A STRANGE COMPUTER!

+   +   +
+

He learnt how to wash his socks and shirt everyday by Fax. The first few times his shirts kept regrouping as swimming trunks.

+   +   +
+

Once a strange cross jumped out of the Fax. Ah, a Maltese cross! He drew his sword and threw himself at our cross. The rivals crossed swords. The stranger was run through and dived into the eternity of the Fax.

+   +   +
+

AH, FAX, THE STYX OF THE XXth C.

+   +   +
+

Sometimes they travelled together.
'Let's dial the Kremlin, and go and have dinner there.'
'You know, the Soviet computers are heavy drinkers. They might let us in, but what if they wouldn't let us out?'

+   +   +
+

Two thousand years passed. 'Oh$\pm$. . . ! $\pm$. . . . Darling . . . – let's go into the bathroom . . .

+   +   +
+

. . . But one day she forgot to put the plug in the bath. The nought was washed down with the water. The cross, who was on duty at the opening, yawned and let the visitor out.

How dark it was! How dark and cold it was in the torrent of soap, of your late-come tears, the discouraged wriggling commas of love, the cholera bacilli.

In the infernal depths he came across a solitary, howling sausage. He noticed a rusted stain in one of the pipes. He pierced the rust, and dived through to the damp plaster, scratched a little hole in the ceiling and, white as a ghost, covered in whitewash, he collapsed on the floor of a huge cellar.

He realised this must be an artist's studio, because there was a broken easel. The artist must have got rich and gone away. He was Russian, apparently, for there was a reel of Soviet black insulating tape lying in the corner.

Soviet tape is no match for Western invisible Scotch tape. There, if your evening trousers are torn, you can stick them together with tape. You can also use it especially on yellow shoes: just stick the Scotch tape on and go off to the reception.

If you're having a wedding reception and you have no pickled herring, cut the tape into thin strips and stick them side by side in the dish. Garnish with sticks of carrots and onion to taste.

The door was locked from the outside. There were no windows. There was no Fax. He had to wait.
In those weeks of waiting he created those pictures from Sellotape that became so famous later. He stuck the tape on the white walls. He created self-portraits and crossings of fate, the shades of the XXth century. Researchers will find many interpretations of the Sellotape

oeuvre, but no one realised that these creations of ISOLating tape arouse out of longing and parting with ISOLda.
Soon he got through all the Sellotape.

He almost went blind, and became completely pale from the dark.
Suddenly the door was thrown open. A crowd of reporters and fans burst in, including the artist himself. 'It was in this hole that I started out'. Then everyone noticed the pictures on the wall. 'These are masterpieces! Why did you hide them from us?' The artist was confused, but he did not reject the works.

The cross crawled out of the open door. Freedom was more important to him than fame and art.

He was homeless. One day when he was wandering around he recognised his self-portrait on a hoarding in the street. He went to the private viewing at the Museum of Modern Art. He could hardly get near the pictures. His reflections were hanging everywhere like mirrors.
'I know the artist!' Blue noughts sparkled in the crowd excitedly. So you saw the adverts too and now you're here. 'The Cross drew this. Look at his mark here on the wall. Here he is himself. Compare the two!
'Yes, it's him!'
The cross put his hand out to her, and they ran out in confusion.

He embraced her round shoulders. Now they were going down the sunny side of Broadway!
A cross and a nought together: it's as though nothing else exists in the world.

Happy ending?

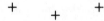

'No!' a painfully familiar voice thundered out of the skies. 'Up your Happy Ending!'

It grew dark suddenly. Isolda, eclipsing the sun with her arse, parachuted down to earth from the sky. She was wearing the striped vest of a paratrooper. Her skirt served as her parachute. She still hadn't managed to get any knickers. Leaflets menacingly fell from her and were carried on the wind to the prairies and pampases. How come she didn't spike herself on the Empire State Building?

+   +

   +

'No!' Isolda threw herself at Audrey. She turned round. The Empire State Building was knocked sideways by the near miss. Fire broke out in the lifts.

+   +

   +

Isolda laid her righteous hands on Audrey in a full nelson. Audrey attempted a 'Lady Hamilton', but it was too late. She couldn't breathe in the powerful Slav embrace.

+   +

   +

'No . . .'
'You beautiful one!' Isolda planted a French kiss on her nought. Let's forget about the knickers! I love you. Let's make our countries friends! The stripes on the paratrooper's vest went red from joy, like the stripes on the American flag.
'Down with the stereotypes of enemies!' 'Long live stereotypes of friendship!' 'Happiness is not having Knickers!' the happy leaflets floated around. 'Naked Friendship'.

+   +

   +

Arm in arm the women went off rustling through the fallen leaflets.

$$\boxed{\text{Audrey} + \text{Isolda} == \text{for ever}}$$

THE CRIME OF THE CENTURY

In the morning Audrey said: 'Are you bored? Why don't you rob a bank?'
The cross decided to rob a memory bank.
He took with him a nought instead of a sack.

+   +   +

They entered the programme code by Fax. 'Nought, where on earth are we?'
'In Purgatory, the torture chamber of the memory,' a loud voice explained.
'O, cross, why did you take this nought with you? One more nought and you'd have dialled the number of Hell.'

+   +   +

They found themselves in a huge clean computer. There were 'rooms' with numbers.
'Petrov, what are you doing here?' He recognised his schoolmate from school 554.
'I'm working on the positive end of the Enter terminal. Here they're always losing their memories, and entering on others' memories and tormenting themselves. You'd better lie low, or they'll find and exchange you.'

+   +   +

Lenin was sitting there. He wanted to take Hope Krupskaya with him, but saw the placard: 'Abandon Hope, all ye who enter her'.

+   +   +

The leader of the Pamyat (Memory) society kept being tormented by the idea of getting out to Israel. Isolda was in convulsions of passion for the Cross.

+   +   +

They all rushed to the door. The doors were like a huge cut-off switch. There was a fiery placard above them: 'Hell is having a free memory.'
'This is a false door. Disinformation. Hell is within us.

58

+   +   +
       +

'Do you think that that's a thermometer on the corner of Gorky Street opposite the post office? Look closer. There are crosses on a stake. They are being tortured. That's why the column is red.'
'But that's disinformation too.'
When the computer gets overloaded with information I throw the cut-off switch. The power is cut off. The whole of world history is destroyed.
Everything is transformed into a current. Hell is a dot. No memory, all information wiped out.

+   +   +
       +

Soon everything will vanish into a dot. Then there'll be another civilisation, of rhomboids and sinusoids. This will be a higher plane of life. But then they'll vanish into a dot.

+   +   +
       +

'Free us of our memory. Cross, you loved us once!' Isolda and millions of martyrs screamed.
The cross stretched out his arms to the whole world.
He began to stuff them all into the nought's sack. The sack puffed out incredibly. It became as big as the globe, and the nought was bursting like the equator. Then suddenly . . .

+   +   +
       +

Everything vanished. It was the nought's son, who had secretly been tracking them, who had laid himself down as an isolating ring between the terminals and cut off the power.

All was lost. Isolda, and millions of memories, everything that is in this book, everything that ever was or would be written, even the meaning of writing – all lost, for ever.

+   +   +
       +

All there was was the little dot of Hell.
The deserted equator rode roughshod over the ruins of civilisation.
It was rolling with laughter.

+   +   +
       +

But it wasn't like that at all. He dialled the number of Hell. He was amazed that absolutely nothing had happened. The room was the same. You were at the Fax machine, and as for Hell . . .
'So this is Hell, then?' 'Yes,' the bathroom mirror replied.
'So it's just the same in Hell as up here.'
   'No, up here it's just the same as in Hell.'
   You laughed and said: 'Are you bored? Let's go into the bathroom.'

The Law of
the Dragonfly

+   +   +

I read the sky and my soul sees more penetratingly.
'I + You' is written all around.
The illiterate builders, when they'd finished their work,
left a cross in the sky.

'Hawk + cloud' is written in the area.
Hill + town. Distance + distance.
+ golden unknown,
+ luminous sadness.

And towards evening Moon + Sun,
underlined by the lines of wheat.
'I + You' hang over the horizon.
'Sky + I = love.'

The Cross and the Sickle

Let us light the candles of forgiveness
for 25th February,
so that Erevan and Fergana
can breathe a little easier.

You were born in the sheep fold,
where the dung is like a rosary.
Let us light the candles of forgiveness.
They who haven't lit them cannot understand us.

The Muslim crescent moon drew close,
like a lacquered nail's edge,
over the temple, too distant for vengeance,
to the place where the cross was on high.

The Hammer and the Sickle are the emblems of vengeance.
The Cross and the Sickle are the covenant of compassion.
Resurrection means forgiveness.
There is no other resurrection.

After the Tone

'I am an answering machine.
You have one minute at your disposal.
Please leave your message after the tone:'

'It's Alla,
please sign the telegram in support of the Senegal freedom fighters.'
'Give me a ring. I'm feeling really bad.'
'You have one minute at your disposal.'
'You'll answer for Chagall,
you bastard.'
'You have one minute at your disposal.'
'I sent you the poem,
please get in contact with Emma,'
'Record this: I am the voice from beyond,
an information leak from the other side.'
'This is Masha,
the S group invites you
to the old castle.
How are you on Uzbek girls?'
'It's the poets from the "Vertep Robbers" Den'.
'Is that Voznesensky's answering machine?'
'This is Tariverdiev the composer's answering machine.
It's verdict time for our owners.
Long live international solidarity for answering machines.'

'Let's respond to Haile Selassie's machinations!'
'Return the poem,
contact Emma.'
'You have one minute at your disposal.'

I am an answering machine.
I answer
from the Black River to Kamchatka
for the mutilated age of eternal questions,
for radiation in packets of tea . . .
for Parnassian porn, for background noise,

Talmuds, Buddhas, Christs, Judases.
You have one minute at your disposal.
Leave your message after the tone.
After the tone.
Blind
chase AFTER
blindchaseafterblindchaseafterblind
chase intone after THE TONE

In Answer to a Note

Everyone is writing, and I'm stopping.
I wrote about Stalin, Vysotsky, Baikal,
Grebenshchikov and Chagall,
Vishnevskaya and Havel,
Lithuania, Georgia and Memorial,
when it was forbidden.

I don't want to swim in the mainstream.

THERE can be no truer moment
than the chance discovery
of two lovers sleeping, tossed aside
like an unfinished book on its back.

THE SITUATION

This is my shadow cabinet.
There's no wardrobe yet,
or the full works of that boring playwright Calderon.
I've been buying this Tsar Alexander sideboard
on hire purchase for several years.
Here is a catapulting armchair
from the anti-cult battle.
In the shadow from this icon is
'The filmstar devouring a dragon.'
I promised to give it to a poet.
It's supposed to be
VI century.
Theofan the Greek, the icon painter.
The table with Kent cigarettes.
There's an answer to a survey on the table:
'I prefer Russian "Belomor" to "Kent".'

Here is a water-colour portrait of my wife.
A nude.
A Persian miniature.
III century, purple enamel.
She must be in the dining room . . .
Here is my dining room of shades –
look what a fine room it is!
For dinner
there's everything that can't be bought:
(there follows a list of foods).
The shade of grandmother – a patterned serviette,
which she, in her suffering, sewed, with illusory monograms.
Careful, you'll drop grandfather!
The piano is a Steinway,
it was my mother's.

My wife must have been playing Rachmaninov for us.
One of the keys was still warm
and half depressed.
(He struck it) Oh, what a sad note.
She must be in the bedroom.
She must have heard us and gone to tidy up.

'Turn the light out when you're through.'
'When you come through the door,
please wipe your feet.
The ceilings are new,
please make sure your head's clean.'

This is my bedroom of shades.
Oh, what a mess . . .
It's a good thing my wife's not here.
Shades of Milly, Nadya, Tanya, Ninnette
and fourteen girlies
from the whore strip.
A corner of forgotten things!
Small size,
Medium size,
Extra extra large – no one really admits to it!
Here's my wife's brooch,
and her discarded dress . . .
She must have gone to the Ivanov chemist
for pills . . .
She's an actress, you know.
Excuse these family matters . . .

Here's the bathroom.
That's strange.
There's light under the door. It's locked on the inside.
No I don't believe it! Open up, you pill-popper.
Do you hear the water flooding the floor?
(He knocks.) No answer.
(He changes unrecognisably when the thought dawns.)
O, no, not that, not that!
Let's break the door down!
Only yesterday she was saying:
'If you don't come home . . .'

Darling, what have you done?
(He smashes the door down)
My God!
No one there. Just a misted up mirror.
The empty depths of the flooding bath.
The towels are dry and untouched . . .

A voice from out of the wall:
'Why should I dry myself,
since I've flown into the ventilation system
on my broomstick?'

A little girl in ribbons
bounced crazily between you and me,
living by her six-year-old truth, she screamed:
'You two are married.'

Your answer was like a slap:
'What do you mean I'm married to him?
Why are you looking at me like that?
Ask him for yourself.'

She looked at me trustingly.
She must be joking, it can't be.
Grey eyes of mine in your face
begged not to be killed.

It was all lies, and that's difficult.
Yours and my tears
rolled from your crazed little eyes:
first sharing.

THE OBLIVIOUS ZOMBIE

I woke, sensing I was being looked at. I was staying near the station.
There was a zombie girl, standing by my window.

Some alien force
opened the window.
My oblivious zombie, stood, all in a fever,
knee deep in forgiveness, knee deep in a snowdrift,
with one shoe lost and clutching the other like a bomb.
My zombie, who has forgotten her program.

Her bandaged finger, with a green medicine stain,
had been pricked by a christmas tree tip, like an opened umbrella.

She looked right out of it, standing alongside,
slipping into a dream.
Between me and the garden
stretched a mindless, questioning look
of criminal house-breaking and spiritual collapse.
Have mercy on yourself, deprogram yourself, zombie!
I opened the window. She was trembling but did not come in.
I don't make a hobby of reasoning with pilgrims.
I shut the window. I shouted at her angrily:
'Unblock yourself, zombie! You're a machine, zombie,
as though you're on drugs,
you sleep, get up, and run through the catacombs of the metro,
in zombie crowds, burying yourself in Dickensianism,
studying courses on advertising hoardings –
you'll get your degree soon.
Have mercy on yourself, deprogram yourself, zombie!
I am your master. Give up your rebellion.
Who has blocked your ears with lead earrings?
Stop snivelling. Unblock yourself, zombie!'
I was boorish, no more, no less;
but some eternal will cast me into the black snowy field . . .
Zombies together, we flew over Tambov and Obminsk,
and at nights you didn't scream 'mama',

but below the panorama of the towns repeated after you:
'I've forgotten my program. I've forgotten my Ruby Wax program!'
The incomprehensible force that carried us repeated:
'I've forgotten, I've forgotten something . . .'
We have forgotten the program brought down from the skies,
on our road to earth, in heaven, and wherever.

Have mercy on yourself, deprogram yourself, zombie!
Have mercy on yourself, deprogram yourself, fields!
Deprogram yourself, grey sun,
into the world that muses on love.

Have mercy on yourself, deprogram yourself, zombie.
Time, once you were life, if I'm thinking correctly,
now you have forgotten the code of the commandments,
oblivious zombie.

Deprogram yourself, slipper snowdrop!
Have mercy on yourself, deprogram yourself, train!
This story that I myself did not understand
will turn into life later on.

It's all over. You killed me the next day,
but that's not what I am praying for from over the horizon:
didn't that free you?
Deprogram yourself, my dear zombie.

1982

THE Vladimir madonna,
shining on the white wall,
is like a cinema cashier
in the oval of the window.

Give me
a ticket
for a film,
which is not allowed
for anyone over sixteen.

SERGEI Yesenin and Marina Tsvetayeva,
two 'dead weights',
hang on invisible chains
in the Russian grandfather clock
with the old-fashioned chimes.

It wasn't as though they loved each other particularly.
But these two royal weights of guilt
move the country's time forward
in the midst of electronic alarm clocks.

Dusks and dawns come and go
in time to this sinful pair.
When Tsvetayeva's weight wins
the clock's chimes toll like bells.

Russian American Romance

They sleep till dawn in my country
and in your country; and not back to back.

The same moon is doubly gold,
in my country and in your country.

For you the sunrise and for me the sunset
are priced high for some reason.

You're not to blame, and I'm not to blame
for the dawn cold outside the window.

There is love and pain for our countries
in your lies and my lies.

Come on then, let's chuck out the idiots
from your country and my country.

1977

BLACK AND WHITE

Tavern violins and harps sob your hearts out,
over the black daisy with an Afro haircut,
who has gone to sleep in a bar, leaning on her friend,
and she has been sick over his trousers.

He carried her still sleeping to the toilets.
He thought to himself 'No creature could be so poisoned'.
The wino body flooded with dreams
writhed darkly on the toilet seat.

'O set yourself free! I am on bended knee,
I kiss your shoulder again and again through your damp
                              cotton blouse.
Give back to me in sincerity your essence,
set yourself free. Set yourself free,

from reality that is gloomy, from a secret that torments us,
from music, brazenly bursting out and rising,
from life that has raced past, but cannot ever pass.
Set yourself free, set yourself free.

Set yourself free, o woman who cannot be woken.
I wash you as a baby after childbirth is washed.
Perhaps your essence is unique
and a step towards freedom and years of caring.

Water falls off your Afro ringlets,
like lazy lenses in black frames.
My present is unwanted, my present is in vain:
set yourself free.

ANT

He stowed away in the rowing boat
and crossed the river with me.
They won't accept the ant
from the other side in these anthills.

He's black, with little white balls,
perhaps a little too white.
But he's an ant from the other side,
an ant from the other side.

Coming from the other bank,
he must be like an Old Believer to Catholics,
who have to drag needles
sharp end down not up.

I would ferry you back, my little refugee,
but I cannot spot you in the crowd,
and I don't have the precise bearings
on that other bank either.

The bank with its pinkish
strawberry sides.
Even I don't have the technology
to bring these banks together.

In a month, he'll float back across on a twig
back to his family,
but he'll get the same reception on that side:
'You're an ant from the other side.'

1973

TROUBADOURS AND BURGHERS

Let's face it, our cause is long lost:
you've walked on our corpses
– but though you've survived and destroyed us,
you were always the corpses, while we were the trumpets.

The trumpet of Fate
cried out in the teeth
of history's dumbness
with the chill of the Gods.
You were the cowards, we the trumpets.

You built up walls around us
because we had your women
in ecstasies
– we burst through the thick walls
and sound the trumpets still . . .

We're the troubadours with the fool's touch:
how right you were to trample on us,
to take over every inch of property . . .
You own space
but Time flies with us.

Do you admit to yourselves
in your safe soundproofed mansions
that you envy the trumpet?
Corpses – live again! Trumpets – cry on!

TRANSLATED BY RICHARD MCKANE
WITH MICHAEL HOROVITZ

THE LAW OF THE DRAGONFLY

I lived, not without risk,
in the law of 'on the left' and 'on the right',
in the left-leaning ways,
driven on the right side of the road,
where the law of the powers-that-be
waves a fiery truncheon.
There is only one truth:
the law of self-seek-self.

A Crimean Tartar, forcibly expelled
from his homeland, lying in rags on his deathbed,
as he supped his pigswill soup
from the crescent of his aluminium bowl
granted to me this curse:

but said 'It won't make you happy.'

The snowman and Nietszche
write this on the mountain heights,
on books that read from left to right,
and books that read from right to left,
in the jerk of suicide,
in the self-knowledge of nations
and in the law of God:
self-seek-self
on the lips of the entrepreneurs.

But the crucified palms
of the law of man
showed people the way
either left, or right.

I sought at the crossing
the way of the spirit and the Minsk road.
The purple tear-bottle
of a woman from Samothrace –
wingless but headless – glistened.

In the sky, as a hoarding over a restaurant,
these letters burned into words:
THE LAW OF SELF-SEEK-SELF

And she said: 'Hey, kitten,
the modern maddener madonna
has disproved the law
of postbrigittebardot tits.
What was considered the law
of high risk groups
has become the norm in every home
and in the nomenclatura.
The law of self-seeking
permeates unrequited love,
perverse love,
gay-blue vice,
white hate,
golden separation,
but give me a whisky or I won't go on.'

And a passer-by
in camouflage green
with the corpse of music in a case said:
'What is written on the T shirts?
What is written on the labels
of your labelguard arses?
What is written in the rebel tapes
in the style of rock or disco?
You must overcome dis-
harmony, as Dziga teaches.'

The law of self-seeking –
no, don't confuse it with self-investigation –
is self-demonstrable in everyone,
and punishable by law.

Michelangelo crawled like a fly
painting the Sistine ceiling,
re-versing heaven and hell,
the law self-seek-self.

I lived in the law of Heaven,
sensing Hell's law,
and from our experiences
and the loss of our nearest,
not from our whimperings,
the law of self-seeking
became our axis.
I realised late and only too well,
for a Tartar was lurking with a begging bowl,
that the sense lay not only in searching for the self,
but in direct action on oneself!

She was standing, waiting for it, at the curbside,
watching the traffic stream by,
her brow furrowed with a new idea.
She was frowning at the wheels.
A little emerald dragonfly
was stuck to her crimson cheek
like a label.

And the cars, God forgive them, flew past.
What were you looking for in them? 'A prince
in dad's limousine? Or a daddy
with a wad of greenbacks?
And why didn't I go up to her?
You stood there, frozen and tense,
for half an hour. Then suddenly, with concentration,
harking back and saying 'go look for me in the river!',
you silently threw yourself under a cab.
I didn't see her writhing
in the squeal of brakes.
Do business with a taxi driver!
Spend some time with a whore?
God forgive these times of prostitution.
God forgive this country, this whore.

Her bloody head bounced
down the road, and the dragonfly sparkled.
What did her little open mouth scream
as the wheel broke off?

No prayers. No notes.
God forgive you, you prostitute.
The little emerald dragonfly
was hovering in the air.

Hey, Dziga, run the film back.
Let the cheek jump back to the dragonfly.
Here's her forehead, and there's her body.
Get up off the road.

Breathe. Car, get back to your garage.
Life, fast-backwards the tape!
'What's your name?' Larissa,
my butt's been on the needle for years.

Life is only a search for the resurrection.

We are standing on the crossroads
of the way of the spirit and the Minsk way.
A student of cinema. A dragonfly girl.
Shadows. A woman with a speech
impediment. A dog with a Mephisto ear,
and a Crimean Tartar.
Horror from the experience,
the dirty funeral wake of a spirit.
I look round and there is a crowd.
They were all looking at the sky;

where burns, like a sign above the doors announcing
that a book is going to be sold on subscription
the perverse cross of life:
SELF-SEEK-SELF

A dragonfly sat on your elbow
and fingered you with its wings
as though its short-sighted eyes
were calmly measuring your skin
like a glass window pane.

Her Story

'I put out the headlights and was driving along slowly.
Where to go? The night was chic.
The bonnet was quivering like a nervous borzoi.
My body was quivering. The night lit the station.
All the impatience of the age of Balzac
bubbled and burned through my skin –
the age of champagne mixed with balsam.

I wound down the left window.

Two young Delons came up to me,
wearing fur coats.'
'Are you free, Miss? Are you willing?
Five hundred an evening, one thousand a night?'

I blushed. They'd taken me for
a prostitute! But my heart beat hard:
'They want you, you're a whore, you're young!'
I was confused. I said 'Yes'.

The other one, unsteady on his feet,
lowering his innocent blue eyes, added:
'Now, if you've got a rich friend like you?
I'll have her for a thousand a night.'

The bastards! Streetwalker kids!
I stepped on the gas, and zoomed off.
But my heart beat sadly and happily!
'Five hundred an evening, one thousand a night?'

To N. N. Berberova

You wrote to me with your left hand,
apologising for your right
which was in plaster – a whiter than white sculpture.

You chose Princeton as a haven,
but what flaked out like snow
on your abandoned plaster arm,
Miss Silver Age?

The maple leaves fell
unclipping like paper clips.
Forgive my right hand
for the fact that it is not in plaster.

Oh Lord, how sweet-smelling
is your suntanned face
that escaped from the secret police.
It's as wrinkled as a peach stone.

How a woman's body once supple
becomes statue and plaster
right in front of my eyes
in gardens we have no knowledge of!

There are nymphs there, summer houses with vistas,
and the Summer Gardens. The oval face of the snow.
The arm that Berberova left behind . . .
Gumilyov was an officer, and as an officer
he walked on her right and took her arm in his.

REQUIEM FOR VYSOTSKY

All Moscow kneels
as Vladimir Vysotsky is laid to rest.
The lyrics of the after–life carried him away
and smoothed his Beatle haircut.

Vladimir died at 2 o'clock,
His full eyes
Were lifeless
as two glasses.
That his moustache grew
was an empty consolation.
The elastic of his underpants cut into him,
smelling of medicine.
Sleep, inveterate chansonnier of all the Russias.
It's our turn to sing at your grave.
Your guardian angel went off
into the skies to have dinner.
Volodya,
if there is blood in the throat,
Volodya,
you turned away
from the clever doctors,
and a peasant woman, a reddish crane,
flying away,
screams over the fabled lands:
'Volodya!'

You walked through sunset Moscow
like a dauber of icons,
with a few drinks in him.
You were more popular than Pele,
with your carefree curls on your brow,
and guitar on your shoulder,
like a pair of halos.
(one big golden one for mother,
and one smaller one for the son).

Volodya . . .
There is a tremor
behind that hoarse voice,
the poisoned hospitality
of melodies,
as though he'd bought a coloured scarf
in the foreign currency shop
that didn't match.
Sleep, serf of the Russian song,
you are free now.
Weep, Russia,
for the golden-tongued slanger-singer!

The time for the Messiah
is eternally here.
Accidents and Emergencies
is New Testament territory.
Risen, he said:
'Shut your mouths.'

The doctors
brought him back to life,
as your song
roared under your mask.
They brought back your grey eyes,
as if they were at a housewarming.
They said: 'Get walking. Honour the land.
Sing more merrily.'
They gave life back to you.
And you, came to,
and said to us: 'You're all going there.
But I'm coming from there!'
Let the orchestras thunder.
Play the trump card, christen him!
Vysotsky is risen,
risen indeed.

1971

FOUL WEATHER

The rain was almost out of Genesis.
I was shoving the car that had got stuck
in the ditch with a wonderfully strong young man.
His face was a mixture of harmonious Russian features
and those of a Byzantine ikon.
The car spat mud in his face
in return for being pushed out.
The clinging liquid lashed us
from under the red brake lights like a pressure hose,
and the wheels skidded
as though they had given up.
I don't really remember whether
my eyes were blinded by that wonderful young mud.
The owner of a writer's dacha
politely brought us towels.
Our saviour washed himself, wiped his hands,
and laughed it off and joked.
Our driver was a blonde friend,
nimble and unskilled.
Solzhenitsyn and I got out together at the outskirts of the city.
Where the wet streets crossed, we parted:
I to the left, he to the right.

1972

Victims

It was not I who killed the ones who could not fight back,
but it terrifies me,
that my fellow citizens killed
them in our own country.

This wasn't happening in Chile.
There was a lump in everyone's throat.
That gas, that teargas,
burst on us all.

I saw Pushkin tear off his top hat,
and walk, through the soldiers ranks,
in a state of shock
to an illegal meeting.

Whether academics or schoolkids
we search for gas
with an anti-perestroika formula:
and it searches us out.

Where is the formula for rubber truncheons
that are against candles?
Those whose fate it was to die,
lie under the Georgian banners.

The candles, crushed by tank tracks,
and a child's look,
forever burn
in the eternal fire of the souls of Georgia.

Unauthorized Meeting

15.IV.89

I repeat that Pushkin would have come
to that unauthorized meeting.
Don't hide behind your umbrellas, like clams!
This is a serious conversation.

We weren't people.
We are ideas,
which have come too late.
Hope came close to
unauthorized suicide.

Unauthorized women
fly through the streets in coffins.
They will never sing again, or cook meals,
or wash their children. There are no children.

It was raining. The unauthorized sun
did not come out on the Arbat.
We are panic, we are the snow in the rain.
The concentration of police
waited for their own panic.
The unauthorized social mind
wants to know – what, when and where?

The formula of the gas was borne on the air
into our dawning minds.
No one pronounced this out loud.
But everyone understood this.

Throw roses in the air for those who've been killed!

Who killed them? Was it the Saracens?
The Arbat was full of soaked people.

We, the tears in the throat of our country,
are unauthorized.

DEMONSTRATION

I walked from a Moscow bridge
in a strange demonstration.
Long live demonstrations
which turn us into monsters!

Balloons of consciousness, raving monsters,
sail over like morse code flashes.
Monsters, let's bear portraits of ourselves
and put them on the heap.

Envy is the moving force of society,
marriage in the party under the lash,
and the growth of the crime rate increases –
monsters, on the heap with you.

Like Sirens, their lower halves
were hidden by the table on the dais.
They're minds were one-track like the Trans-Siberian railway,
and they devoured their colleagues under the counter
and scratched the country with their claws.

Thirteenth apostle in line for his wages
an author carried an Easter placard.
'Foreigners are shits!
as comrade Stalin said.'

We warmed them with our dank souls.
The banner shafts trembled like umbilical cords.
We part with the monsters in tears.
We are to blame for their birth.

The monsters with morals of a monastery
without a God.
Cry, frozen independence,
the Soviet solar plexus system.

My Proposal for a Memorial to the Victims of Repression

Not the pyramids of the pharaohs. Not the pantheons
                    of Rome.
I see a pulsating light visible over the city.
A new name flares up every second.
There are 30 million seconds in the year.

At midnight of 3rd of March, Tabidze's second flashes,
and at 9.15 Mandelstam flashes like lightning,
Ivan Smith, the peasant, has a second to cross himself again,
and a six-year-old girl has a second to breathe.

I see this memorial not in space but in time.
A memorial alarm clock waking the moment.
Let Berggolts be pregnant again for a second.
A comet showers down in a million anonymous seconds.

Let the planes check their speed by a little girl's second.
Let the bastard be forewarned for the future by example.
I want to erect a memorial not in time but in the conscience.
The calculation is in seconds. Conscience is the
                    measure of seconds.

1987

94

THE MADONNA OF 1937

There are women in the Russian cities,
who sweep the chaos out of the country.
Perhaps they are Karate experts,
but there is a sadness in their divine beauty.
The women working on the Russian squares
wear orange coats as they lay asphalt,
so that the shame should be more obvious:
the oranges of our squares!
(But just try and have pity on them!)
Is there anyone in our cities who can understand them
as the rollers crush them?

. . . .

Emaciated by tobacco, Berggolts,
one of the prophetesses, told me a true story,
how her interrogator beat her
till she miscarried, and threw her flying down the stair-well.
She still flies and still she sings
over the country in the fine slanting rain:
'My son!'
Return the woman into my ashes.
Is there anyone in the cities of Russia?

Years later he sat next to her in the Kremlin hall,
and asked joyfully, without a trace of evil:
'Olga Fyodorovna, do you remember me?'
She got up and went off without a word.
The malingering bear, the Saturn of the Russian revolution,
devoured his own children.

Let the women of the cities of Russia
pray to her in childbirth,
14-year-old mothers
hurry to deliver her into the world,
little girls of the same age as Juliet.

She is joyful – but she has no happiness.
Olga! Olga! You look young,
Madonna of 1937.
Can one begin to forget that shame and terror?
Is there anyone in the cities of Russia?

THE prisoners make the seat-covers for Aeroflot.
My flights are solidly based on their crimes,
both minor and terrible. The prisoners
sew the material for the seats from strong cloth,
so that we can catapult into flight.
I cannot sleep in the section with the blinds down.
A rapist bit this thread with his teeth.
A framed woman prisoner ruined her eyesight.
Prisoners sew the seat-covers for Aeroflot.
I pray for an unknown woman prisoner,
who swore as she sewed this chair-cover for me.
Oh Lord has she died or is she risen again?
Sky. Freedom. Thighs of the Gods.
Prisoners sew the seat-covers for Aeroflot.

HIPPODROME

Did the Bronze Horseman ever undergo
a doping test?

The needle of the Admiralty Spire
gleams unobtainably.

SLEEP, my little one. How terrible the times are!
The shadows under your young eyes
trembling slightly from your light dreams –
they are the shadows of the future coins on your lids.

A Cut-Diamond Fable

Oh Lord, have mercy on the miscalculated deviations
of your servants.
A forgotten spirit is in the air –
is he a doorman or the General Secretary?
The Order of Victory (in transition)
with diamonds extracted,
as though a plate for false teeth
left lying on the sideboard.

Who owns these diamonds?
The millions who fell for them?
He stuck rigidly to the régime
and was the zombie of a sick epoch.
He was inexorably
tied in to the alarm system.

The diamond generals
courted his daughter.
They, who fawned over his daughter,
are now attacking Brezhnev himself.
She wanders, empty-eared
over the billiard table,
the tormented toy
of glittering tricksters,
and no longer hears the balls click.

Her diamonds, that blazed
like rockets at a firework display have vanished.
The diamond general drove
the Mercedes into and through the Red.
The capital lies
on the snow
with its extracted
domes.
And the extracted talents
gaze
from exiled
skies.

YOUR plane disappeared behind the mountains.
The sun was setting, and the moon rose
at a slant. The storm was approaching.
Two paths flared up on the water,
like two springs from a mattress,
one red and one of steel.
They were whisking egg whites for the devil.
I walked along the shore, but could not get away from them.
The two spiralling paths whirled.
I lay on my back. The sand was stifling hot.
I heard the dance music from the restaurant.
A rock group was playing 'Salmonella'.

For Belka and Strelka

Hey Russia,
you're all in the dark.
There's a doggy smell
up in the sky.

Over topsails, powerstations,
masts, antennae and factory chimneys,
the corpse of a dog
rushes through the atmosphere
in the terrifying Sputnik
of Progress.

1959

Ditch

A Spiritual Process

AFTERWORD

On 7 April 1986 I was driving with some friends along the Feodosia highway from Simferopol. The clock on the taxi dashboard showed ten in the morning. Vasily Fyodorovich Lesnykh, the driver of our taxi, a man in his sixties, heavy, with a ruddy, windblown complexion, and blue eyes that had faded from what he had seen, kept repeating his harrowing story. Outside the town, here at the tenth kilometre, 12,000 peaceful inhabitants, of Jewish nationality, were shot.

'Well, us lads – I was ten then – ran to watch how they were shot. They brought them in covered lorries. They stripped them to their underclothes. There was an anti-tank ditch running from the highway; they just mowed them down with machine-gun fire above the ditch. They were all screaming terribly, and their groans hung over the steppe. It was December. They'd all taken off their galoshes and thousands of them were strewn about. Carts were going past on the highway, but the soldiers did not stop them. The soldiers were all drunk. When they saw us they gave us a burst of fire. Oh yes, I remember there was a little table where they collected the passports. Passports were scattered over the whole steppe. Many were buried while still half alive. The earth breathed.

'Later we found a shoe-polish box in the steppe. It was heavy, and in it was a gold chain and two coins, all the family savings. So they'd taken with them all their valuables. Later I heard that someone had discovered this burial place and dug up the gold. They were tried two years ago. But you know about that anyway.'

My friends had stolen archive materials for me, which was forbidden. I had interviewed witnesses. My poem was finished, but wouldn't go out of my mind. I was drawn again and again to the scene of destruction. But what would I see there? Just kilometre after kilometre of overgrown steppe.

'I have a neighbour called Valya Perekhodnik. He was probably the only survivor. His mother pushed him off the lorry as they were being taken there.'

We got out of the car. Vasily Fyodorovich was visibly upset.

A wretched, cracked, once-plastered column with an inscription about the victims of the invaders stood there, and spoke more about oblivion than memorial.

'Shall we take a photo?' my friend said getting out his camera. The cars streamed down the road. The young shoots of emerald wheat stretched to the horizon. On the left a tiny farm cemetery nestled idyllically on the rise. The ditch was green and had long ago been levelled, but its outline could be seen, coming across from the highway for about one and a half kilometres. Shy branches of blackthorn blossomed white, and the occasional dark acacia stood out.

The sun made us sleepy as we walked slowly down the highway.

Suddenly – what's that? There was a black square of a freshly-dug shaft on the path among the green field; the earth was still damp. Alongside there was another. There were rotted clothes around a mass of charred bones, and smoke-blackened skulls. 'They're digging again, the bastards!' Vasily Fyodorovich had been right.

This was not on documentary film, nor in the stories of witnesses, nor even in a nightmare: it was right here and now. It was all freshly dug up. One skull after another. Two tiny children's ones, and an adult's, smashed into fragments. 'They prise the gold crowns off with pliers, you see.'

A battered woman's shoe. Oh my God, hair and a scalp, a child's red hair in a plait! How tight it was plaited as though they were hoping for something that morning before they were shot . . .

This is not a literary device, these are not heroes that have been dreamed up, or the pages of a criminal investigation – we are standing alongside the busy highway in front of a heap of human skulls. Our people, yes our people of today did this, not evil monsters of antiquity. What a nightmare! They were digging last night. A broken filter cigarette is lying on the ground. It's not even damp. Alongside is a brass cigarette case that's turned green. 'German', Vasily Fyodorovich says. Someone picks it up, but throws it down immediately – there's a danger of infection.

The skulls were lying in a heap, those enigmas of creation, dark-brown from long years underground, just like huge smoked mushrooms.

The professionally dug shafts were about twelve feet deep, and in one there was further digging. A shovel with dust on was half-hidden at the bottom of the other. So they're going to come and dig again today!

We looked at each other in horror and disbelief. It was all a terrible dream.

How far can man go, how depraved can his mind be, to dig among skeletons, by the side of a busy road, to crush skulls and prise off crowns with pliers by the light of headlights? Among them was a young woman, who was pregnant and was digging with a baby in her womb! They made rings out of the gold teeth of the murdered and wore them. And furthermore to conceal virtually nothing and leave everything in evidence so demonstratively, almost as a challenge. As for the people driving calmly down the highway, they would just grin and say: 'Somebody's digging for gold again.' Has everyone gone out of their minds?

There was a tin sign stuck on a stake next to us: 'Digging is prohibited – cable.' So you can't dig up a cable, but you can dig up people? So even the court procedures did not make this bastard stop and think, and as I was told later they only talked at the trial of the perpetrators of the crime and not the fate of those they buried there. And what is the epidemic station doing? All sorts of infections could emerge from those shafts. An epidemic could decimate the region. Children run wild over the steppe. And what about a spiritual epidemic?

The fresh lilies-of-the-valley bloom in the grass. I bend down. It's the bones of a child's little finger, washed clean by last year's rain and floods. The police patrol the highway for speeders and fines, but do not look over here. They should have a post here. One for 12,000.

12,000 are worthy of this. The four of us are standing at the tenth kilometre. We are ashamed and we cannot find the words to express what should be done. Perhaps grass should be laid, and paving stones with a border round. Just call out and the best sculptors will erect a stele or marble plaque, to send a sacred shudder down people's backs. Then names should be remembered. We don't know what should be done, but something should be done fast.

That's how I was confronted with last year's Case No. 1586 which rose again.

Ditch, where are you leading to?

It was very difficult to get this poem published. This was all before glasnost. The magazine *Yunost* took the risk. I received about 900 readers' letters, in shock at the crime in the Crimea. There were also a few anti-Semitic letters.

Many more of them started to come when I wrote about Chagall, who had been banned, before I went to Vitebsk to try and found a museum. One could see from these letters the growth of anti-Semitism in our country. Ditch, where are you leading to?

I will give just one example. When I was performing in the October concert hall, I received a note about *Ditch*: 'Go suck a dead Rabbi's prick', and they had in mind a Rabbi, murdered by the Nazis. The director of the concert hall had warned me beforehand that members of the *Pamyat* society had bought 200 tickets and were sitting in the third and fourth rows. (There were 2,000 people in the hall.) Within half an hour I got another picture in a note to the stage, in which a powerful, presumably Slav, member was bursting through a Star of David.

My anger goaded me to read better and better. When the hall was chanting for more, I stopped the applause and said: 'My friends, there's glasnost up here on stage but not among you.' 'Why?' the third and fourth rows roared. 'Because I answer your notes honestly, but you don't sign your notes. Let's take one at random. Well, for instance, who is the artist of this anti-Semitic pornography? Stand up! There's democracy now, you won't be arrested.'

I showed the picture of the prick to the audience. Silence. The black hall was silent. No one stood up.

Then I shouted: 'You're cowards, cowards, cowards!'

The 2,000-seater hall clapped. The pogromists were afraid. They had lost. That was then, but how about tomorrow? Ditch, where are you leading to?

Ten minutes later a confident woman made her way up to the stage of the October hall. (I was told later that she was the press attaché of *Pamyat*.) She said to me: 'Just so you don't think we are cowards, I want to present you with our manifesto,' and she gave me a brochure which laid out scientific proof that the Jews had destroyed Russia.

Ditch, where are you leading to?

Introduction

I address the skulls of my readers:
have we run out of reason?
We are standing in the steppe.
A dusty highway in the Crimea.
My skull jumped under my scalp.

Alongside, a black one,
blackened, like a smoked mushroom.
It harboured a grin in its little fist.

I sensed
a certain secret connection –
as though I was hooked into a conversation
that stretched away from us
to eyeless cameras,
like a cordless telephone.

'Hallo, Alla Lvovna!'
'Mama, we're trapped . . .'
'Storms again, and cosmic interference . . .'
'Real Hitchcock, kitsch!'

Skulls. Tamerlane. Do not open the graves.
War will burst from them.
Do not cut the mushrooms
of the souls with the spade.
Something more terrible than the plague will emerge.

What sort of a poet are you, 'voice of the people'?
Is your bread rising?
Before the eyes of twelve thousand pairs of eyes,
stop chattering and do something!

Wherever I've gone,
whatever I've read,
I still go into that Simferopol ditch.
And the skulls, the black skulls, float
like an eclipse of white minds.

And when I go to Luzhniki Stadium even,
each time now I will see
the pupils of twelve thousand pairs
of eyes making their demands.

Ditch

Fate, do not drag me
into the Simferopol ditch.
Steppe. The twelve thousandth look.
Listen! to the clank of spades
of the patriotic grandsons.
Genocide laid down this treasure.

'Don't dig!'
'We were people.'
'Here, take it! I've brought a diamond.'
'Stop shaking so, Dad.
Give up your treasure, then get back to sleep.'

It is good for people to
be the first to find happiness.
But God forbid that you be the first
to see this fresh pit
where the skull is dug up.
Valya! This was your mother.

This is fact not fiction,
fact not fiction,
gold dust, bone dust.
The vampire takes the bracelet off the skeleton,
and someone else drives off.

This is far away, far away,
far, far away.
A skull, the night, and the flowering almond tree.
The internal *pogromer*
calmly put his foot down
on the spade and then the gas pedal
The metal spade rang.
Who's hit his own skull,
but not realized it in the dark?

Hamlet, gaunt and emaciated,
held the skull
and prised off a row of crowns.
Man is different from the worms.
The worms do not eat gold.

Ditch, where are you leading us to?
No flowers, no orphans.
This is genocide – the graveyard of souls.
A blizzard of passports whirls over the steppe.
And no one brought hyacinths.

LEGEND

The Angel of Death comes after your soul,
like a terrible opened-out, three-leaved mirror.
I read in ancient legends
that he is made all of numerous eyes.
Did not Christ or Shestov the philosopher know
why he had such numerous eyes?

If he is mistaken
(for your time is calculated)
he flies away, leaving new sight.
He gives the startled soul
a new pair of eyes.
They say this happened to Dostoyevsky.

You're still on earth,
Valentin, Valentin!
Your mother angel not only saved you,
but gave you the vision of the graves
of twelve thousand pairs of eyes.

And you walk through the plain
with the pain of your new vision.
How your new sight tortures you!
Your breast is not badged with blood
but with the clairvoyant sores of pupils.
And your shirt is rough like haircloth.

You scream in the night,
and see the roots of the cause.
In the morning you look in terror in the triple mirror.
But when that other one
flies in for your soul,
you will not give him your eyes.

Not on the wing of the seraphim,
carried along like a windsurfer
did he cut out and rip out my tongue.
The angel, Valya Perekhodnik,
drives me without a word
to the Simferopol ditch.

An Olive Branch

Debt

History is really
a pitful of debts.

Napoleon owes me
the Arbat, which was burnt down.

Let's imagine that there was no Tartar yoke,
then everything moves 300 years.

Chengiz Khan
owes me the Trans Siberian Railway that was not built 300 years ago.

How about if we'd stormed the Winter Palac in 1617?
The Red and the white roses would have been warring in Europe,
and our State farms would have been flourishing.
If there'd been no Tatar yoke,
Ivan the Terrible would be crawling out of a MIG jet,
and Shakespeare would have come to us to fight for peace.
He'd have taken a carriage to the frontier,
then the Red Arrow Express from Leningrad.

To continue:
I am indebted
to the unread poet Ivan Smith.
I owe
the child of the year 2,000
his gas and electricity bills,
and the dead fish from the north,
(he thanks me for this!)

Will they bring buttercups to celebrate
the 100th Anniversary of the scientific technical revolution?

Farewell to the Microphone

The theatre has given itself up to entertainment.
The crowds are breaking down the doors.
But I am walking off the stage,
walking off the stage.

I, microphone man,
sing to you of the whole century.
They call me the Twentieth Century,
and I am walking off the stage.

And with me go off towns,
stereosystems,
our red experience is the colour of shame,
of the science of *nota bene*,

and of the loneliness in the horde –
you will walk off to there –
the stage will walk off
into the microphone years.

On it there was a breath of change
even in the stifled years.
The leaders shrieked: 'Get off!'
And I walked onto the stage.

I was not born for the stage.
The logic cannot be explained.
The stadium is breathing nearby,
like lungs to be transplanted.

We laid down the sense of music
in uncensored sparkling spectacles
on the only stage in the land
not subjected to censorship.

It still rings in our ears even now.
Sing, bird, there are no bars on your cage!
But the stage
where nothing is forbidden bores me.

I shall come to you again and again
and plead with you.
We can't live without us!
I am walking off the stage.

I love the rust on your constructions
like the legs of the sirens.
But I am walking off the stage,
walking off the stage.

We are rushing to the border of naked writing.
There is no stage there for any values.
But I am walking off the stage,
walking off the stage.

I am grateful to you, stage, that you gave life
and embraced me as well,
and lifted me onto your wings,
that are called Time.

But in new dreams where night is and God is,
I shall dream of looking down on the stage,
and there will be a yolk with a black dot,
and that will become a bird.

THE LITURGY OF YEARS

'Lord, have mercy on me,
Lord have mercy on me.
Praise the Lord in glory and honour.'

The Afghan 'vets' fly in coffins,
Nagorno Karabakh just cannot heal.
Is this not a terrifying vengeance?
The millenium of old Russia,
the millenium of the soul.
Time now for it to be resurrected.

Have mercy on this country,
on the people released into consumerism . . .
Whence has this chorus entered our soul?
Sch-ism. The tyrants' eyes bulge.
Russia has burnt itself in suicide.
There is a black box for the soul.

The soul rushes and prays:
'Yakov have mercy on me . . .'
'Let us praise the despot in glory and honour.'
Places of worship explode. Salvos.
Witnesses are liquidated.
There is a black box for the soul.

In that black box
are the groans of Christ the Saviour,
the displacement of souls weighs a thousand tons,
and the abandoned child
still asks as he looks:
'What's in that black box?'

Soul, have mercy on me,
light the named candles,
for we are all indirectly sinners,
for we have forgotten the soul,
and it aches and screams out:
'I am the black box of the soul.'

People sit in soft armchairs.
People look at the black boxes.
Let us praise the palms that did not live the lie!

The people's planet will burn up.
The black box of the soul
will fly between the Milky Ways.

1987

HAVE you prayed tonight, birch tree?
Have you prayed tonight,
far-flung lakes
Senezh, Svityaz and Naroch?

Have you prayed tonight, cathedrals
of the Protection of the Virgin and of the Assumption?
I'll have a last smoke by the fence.
You need to pray for success.

There is a stink of exhaust fumes
on the scythed meadows . . .
Have you prayed, Russia?
How we loved you before we murdered you.

THE mount of decision. The mount of suffering.
The East is at my back.
A secret chain of crosses
shows through the Mount.

Over there he will stop fifteen times,
falling to the stones,
like kisses strewn over a body
lips on lips.

He will go out to limber up on the mount
and on the second mount
he will see the shadow of the cross
as though in a mirror.

The star in the heavens beats down on his back,
casting a shadow on a cloud:
he was nailed to the sky,
and says from generation to generation:

'Peter denies me.
I take the form of the cross
which costs me a stern discipline.
The lines of light will stretch
into the cosmos and the Siberian Gulag.

Disciples,
why are you crying?
It was my decision.
There's no going away.
The template of my suffering
will chart
the road
for mankind.'

25 OCTOBER 1989

AN OLIVE BRANCH

I am on the downslope
of my years on earth,
looking down from the Mount of Olives.
It's me, Lord.
The cock's crow
became the church's eggshell dome,
it is You, Lord.
O Lord, here I am,
cursed at,
exhaust fumes all around me.
It is you, Lord,
with me in the windswept cafés of Jerusalem.
I hear my father's voice
above the ravine.
The chalice of the chasm
is irreversible –
it is You, o Lord.
Father, I have carried out your programme,
but I am still warm
and have bones in my body.
I used my soul as a witch's broom,
and swept with it.
O Lord, please accept
this 'socialist' pilgrim.
It's me, o Lord, and my people,
who have buried faith
and shit on the cosmos.

The olives are blinded by cars.
The embraces of the Russian Magdalen
are round as domes in the twilight,
and cast a ring around
the feet of the Mount.

A terrible road meandered in the sky
like the shrubs of a bridge across the Moscow river.
The shadow of the cross
stumbled and ate into the stones.
Life's path is nearing
the highest point.
And the olive leaves,
the size of these lines
are recording it all.

I am God's branch
from a Northern valley,
where the Russian huts hunch.
The presence of an
unconquerable love:
this is You, o Lord.

My mistake was that
I lived as a wolf
among wolves:
that was me, o Lord.
But all that I sang
of in my poems,
from 'A to Z':
this is You, o Lord.

JERUSALEM
MOUNT OF OLIVES
26 OCTOBER 1989

Three Prose Pieces

The Poet and the Tsar

The black box of my memory wheezed, burst out in obscene language, spat on itself. A celluloid little blockhead jumped out of it.

The blue, domed Sverdlovsk hall in the Kremlin was rustling, as it filled with ceremonial suits and squeaking nylon shirts, which were in fashion at the time. The crowd was made up mainly of officials with a cautious additional mixture of creative intelligentsia. There were about six hundred people. It was the 7th of March 1963.

The rostrum for those who were speaking was with its back to the presidium table, almost butting on to it and a little lower than the table where reared up Khrushchev, Brezhnev, Suslov, Kosygin, Podgorny and Kozlov, Polyansky, Ilichev. Their ten-metre-high portraits adorned the streets on holidays. They were borne aloft in the demonstrations.

We connected the beginnings of liberalism with Khrushchev. The shoots of glasnost were driving the apparatchiks mad. We already knew from the official press who would be worked over at the meeting in the Kremlin. An article 'The Tourist with a Cane' had already appeared in *Izvestiya*, whose editor was the son-in-law of Khrushchev, as had a special article critical of Ehrenburg. *Izvestiya* again had attacked in an editorial my poems printed in *Yunost*. We had got used to continually being slanged. I thought that Khrushchev was being deceived and that one could explain everything to him. On the first day of the session Khrushchev was sullen, and irritated and kept on interrupting the grey-haired film-director M. I. Romm. They attacked Ehrenburg, and more and more frequently as if by scenario, my name and Aksyonov's began to be mentioned. A. Prokofiev and A. Malyshko were especially zealous against me cackling against me their own 'triangular pears' [from a title of a book by Andrei Voznesensky. Tr.] and driving the nails home. They were winding Khrushchev up. He pretended to be dozing.

This is how M. I. Romm remembers that session.

'Two speeches were key ones, I would say. One was an accusation,

couched in honeyed terms, that Voznesensky had given an interview
in Poland in which he was asked how he related to the older generation
etc., and to generations in literature. He had answered that he did not
divide literature by the horizontal into generations but by the vertical
and for him Pushkin, Lermontov and Mayakovsky were contempo-
raries and belonged to the younger generation. But he added to the
names of Pushkin, Lermontov and Mayakovsky those of Pasternak
and Akhmadulina. As a result a big scandal broke out. I think that was
on the second day.'

V. Vasiliyevskaya was the first one, I think, to trump my term 'the
vertical generation'. They did not understand completely but people
were obviously upset. It was only recently that Pasternak had been
hounded and driven out. Semichastny, at Khrushchev's orders, had
screamed that Pasternak was 'worse than a swine'. 'A swine wouldn't
do what he'd done . . . He's shat in the trough.' In the tumult of the
writer's trial in the Union of Writers, the orators added to the scenario:
'Mister Pasternak, get the hell out of the country!' And then suddenly
that same Pasternak was named not along with swine but with
Pushkin . . .

Here the head of state pretended that he had woken up, and in a
strange high-pitched voice of a fat man called me up to the rostrum.
He was our hope then, and I went up there to tell him freely about the
state of literature, thinking that he would understand everything.

But hardly had I started making my speech when someone from the
presidium behind started interrupting me. I didn't turn round but
continued talking. Behind my back there was a roar on the micro-
phone: 'Mister Voznesensky!' I requested that I not be interrupted and
tried to keep talking 'Mister Voznesensky,' there was a roar, 'get the
hell out of our country, get out!' In those days everyone was called
'comrade' and the usage of 'Mister' was defamatory and used for
enemies.

From the, at first bewildered and then triumphant, faces in the hall,
crowded with the nomenclatura, I sensed that something terrifying
was going on behind my back. I turned round. A few metres away
from me the sweaty face of Khrushchev, disfigured with anger, was
howling at me with the yellow whites of his eyes rolling. The head of
state jumped to his feet, waving his fists above his head in the air. He
was out of control. Sweat streamed over him: 'Mister Voznesensky!
Get the hell out! You are slandering Soviet authority. Get the
f. . . .ing hell out of the country! Out! Comrade Shelepin will see

your passport's ready!' There followed a monstrous torrent of words.
'You want a Hungarian revolution here? Out!' I did not mis-hear: he
screamed not 'counter-revolution', but 'revolution'. Khrushchev
continued: 'We're not those who were in Petofi's Hungarian club,
we're those who broke up that band of criminals. Your actions speak
of anti-Sovietism, anti-party-line! Out! You and your like are not the
thaw or the spring frosts. We'll bring about the cruellest frost.'

'He's out of his mind, perhaps he's drunk?' passed through my
mind. (This happened once when he'd taken his shoe off and banged it
on the table at the United Nations.) It was only force of habit that had
innured me to anything happening when I was performing that made
me hold on to reason. From the hall, to which my back was now
turned, there began a powerful chanting: 'Down with him! Shame!' A
disgustingly handsome face popped up in the first row: 'He comes to
the Kremlin, without a white shirt, without a tie! Beatnik!' Later I
found out that this was Shelepin, who was then head of the KGB. Not
many of those who were there would know the word 'beatnik', but
they picked it up immediately and chanted 'Beatnik! Shame!'

'Ideas, and the party line' were the leitmotifs of the attack. My
special crime was that I declared I was not in the party, and also that I
referred to Mayakovsky. Many people there suddenly realized that
Mayakovsky had not been a party member. They were angry and
upset. Here is the stenographer's record of Khrushchev's speech in the
hall: 'He is challenging us with his: "I am not a party member!" There
is nothing courageous in that! We'll stamp on everyone who opposes
the Communist party. We'll stamp on them! We'll never give freedom
to our enemies, never! Who are you anyway? He wants to create a
party of non-party members. You are a member of a party but it's not
ours. You are slandering the party. Just wait, we'll teach you. No
thaw, but frost. We proposed to Pasternak that he leave the country.
Get your passport and clear off to your people there.'

Voznesensky: 'I am a Russian, why should I leave my country?'

'You are another Pasternak! The party alone will continue to fight
to represent the old and young generation.'

As I looked round the presidium my eyes met the icy stare of
Kozlov. Both he and the other members of the presidium were
looking right through me. How could I stop this nightmare? My voice
somehow got through the general roar and I said that I would read
some poems.

Just then my sleeve caught on a glass and it rolled along the rostrum.

I caught it and held it in my hand. I remember now the cross-shaped facets of the Kremlin crystal glass. I remember how attentively and cautiously Kozlov looked at my hand holding the glass.

'No poems! We know all about them. Off with him!' Screams broke out. The hall was thirsting for blood.

In the screwed up face of the head of state I saw just then that a thought or half a thought was penetrating, as though something had snagged him and awoken his conscience, something was annoying him – or did I just sense this? – as though he saw in the triumphant roar of the crowd his own future demise, and he felt the elemental force of the crazed and out-of-control nomenclatura. Within a year they would wring his neck. Like a wounded bull he bellowed: 'Let him read.'

> What ash-strewn ice age
> has shackled my home land?
> What would my tortured Muse
> sing of in the camp zones?
> . . . when iron-shod and all powerful
> shoes clamber onto the mournful rostrums
> to be beaten there!
> Red stripes on uniforms will stream
> stickily and dangerously . . .

The hall fell into a malicious silence. Those days the head of state, when he lost control over the process put politics on the back burner. As usual when I read, I beat out the rhythm with my upraised right hand. When I finished there was some timid clapping which died immediately. 'He's an agent! An agent', Khrushchev shouted. The thought flashed into my mind that if he was calling me an agent they'd pick me up immediately. He carried on howling, but in a lower tone, as though he was running out of steam. 'Why are you raising your hand? Why are you raising your hand? Are you showing us the way? Do you think you're a leader? Just one thing, you should stop thinking that you were born a genius.'

Voznesensky: 'I never thought that.'

Khrushchev: 'Yes you do. Your talent has gone to your head, well, be happy prince and let the forest greet you. If you don't want to be in step with us, get a passport and leave.'

He was soaked with sweat from his half hour of shouting, and his shirt clung to him in dark patches.

But he didn't even think of pausing.

'Agent, you come here! You with the glasses on! No not you, you with the red shirt, you imperialist agent.' He pointed his short fat finger at the corner of the hall, where the young graphic artist Hilarion Golystin, a student of Favorsky, was sitting. It was he who had applauded me.

Gaunt, melancholic, thoughtful, honest Hilarion, completely not of this world, went up to the rostrum.

'Why did you clap?'

'I clapped Voznesensky because I like his poems.'

'Oh yes, but we can clap and not clap when we shouldn't. And who else do you like?'

(After a pause for thought) 'I like Mayakovsky's poems.'

'How can you prove that?'

(After a pause for thought) 'I can quote them.'

'Why did you come up to the rostrum?'

(After a pause for thought) 'You asked me to.'

'Well since you're here, speak.'

'I didn't come prepared to speak. I don't know what to say.'

'Who are you anyway?'

(After a pause for thought) 'I am Golitsyn.'

'Prince Golitsyn?' (Laughter)

(After a pause for thought) 'I am an artist.'

'Ah, an artist! An abstract artist!'

(After a pause for thought) 'No, I am a realist.'

'How can you prove that?'

(After a pause for thought) 'I could bring my work in to show you . . . My father died in prison. He's been rehabilitated.'

'You're taking vengeance on us because of your father?'

'No, I'm not. Who could do that?'

'Next!'

He dealt swiftly with V. Aksyonov next. He was exhausted. He announced a break.

Later Ehrenburg asked me: 'How could you stand it? Anyone in your situation would have been in shock, even had a heart attack. You can't tell with nerves. It would have been forgivable for you to ask for mercy.'

I remember dimly how he had spoken once and praised Stalin and added some hopeless verses. I remember going through the animated crowd that were smacking their lips. There was suddenly empty space around me, recent friends turned away and vanished.

I remember going out on to the dark March square by the Kremlin. The wind chilled the bone. The slippery pools of light from the streetlamps played on the wet cobblestones which were set close together like the grins on the faces. Where to go?

Someone put a big hand on my shoulder. I looked round and recognized a poet. We were not close, and did not meet often after this, but he came up to me and said: 'Come back to my place. We'll have some tea and drown these troubles.' He forcibly took me away, and did not leave me alone. All night he was occupied with his collection of ikons, trying to play down the nerves. There were only olives to eat in the house. As he filled the little glasses he said:

'The whole power of the country was behind him – all the rockets, the cosmos, the army. It all fell on you. And you, you little blade of grass, you withstood it all. Ah, well . . .'

For a year I went round the country, making myself scarce. I heard there had been meetings where I had been picked to pieces, and there were demands for my recanting, and there were articles. One of the poets who branded me from the rostrum of the Writers' Union demanded the death penalty for me and my friends, as traitors to the home land. At the Latvia railway station I came across a placard, made by Agit-placard, where an angry Worker and a Collective Farm woman were sweeping with an iron broom spies and a certain book (of mine) *The Triangular Pear* out of the country. The placard was signed: 'Fomichev, artist, Zharov text'. Such a placard, only enlarged to huge dimensions, stood at the entrance to Yalta. But the simple people both in Vladimir and in the Baltic states were very good to me then.

Up and down the country they sought out and branded 'their Voznesenskys'. I. Drach and O. Suleymenov got it badly.

My consciousness became numb. I got depressed. But I was young and I got over it. The poetry remained. An American journalist phoned my mother who hadn't known where I was and what was going on with me for six months, and said: 'Is it true that your son has committed suicide?' My mother fainted with the receiver in her hand. Within a year, Khrushchev, who was retired on a pension, got a message to me that he was sorry about what had happened and my being hounded afterwards and that he had been fed disinformation. I answered that I was not angry with him, and that the important thing was the freeing of the people after 1956. It's strange that despite what I had been through, I held no rancour for him – then or now. For a long time I could not work out how the hopes of the sixties, the powerful sweep of transformations, and the brake of the old thinking and a petty merchant's stupid mentality could be combined in one man. But, it's true that I did not sign his seventieth birthday greeting, when he, as head of state, was in his full power, and the Editors of *Yunost* had to sprinkle the signatures not in alphabetical order lest it appear that not everyone had signed. But that involved my feelings of what was right to do.

Yes, the memoirists are right: having passed through the school of acting, of keeping control of oneself, when he hid his hatred for the tyrant, he was forced to dance a Cossack dance in front of guests, and he in his turn took revenge for his old humiliations, and when he came to the throne he himself got into the habit of humiliating people, trampling on their rights. He trampled on the slender poet Margarita Aliger, the old woman Shaginyan; he screamed 'Mister paederasts!' at the artists in the Manège, and the persecution sanctioned by him gave Dudintsev a heart attack. He did not trust the intelligentsia, and was afraid of glasnost. But was he to blame? The black System was to blame, that brought him up. It has been published now, that when he came to power, his first act was to destroy the document about his participation in bloody reprisals. Bloodshed oppressed him, so the feat of his speech at the Twentieth Congress was all the braver.

Historians still have to write a portrait of N. S. Khrushchev and his great deeds, I have only told about one episode, of what I saw and went through. Even at the onset of glasnost *Ogonyok* was not able to penetrate the censorship for almost a year and print Romm's memoirs about the meeting with Khrushchev.

M. Romm wrote about this episode in his memoirs:

'When there was some verbal battle going on, while Voznesensky was trying to answer, suddenly Khrushchev did not interrupt him but turned to the hall and shouted to the back seats: "Why are you grimacing like that? You with the glasses on in the last row, in the red shirt!" And about my ill-fated reading of poems: "He reads but he can't get through." Khrushchev is banging his fists on the table behind him. The icy Kozlov is by his side. He read a long poem. Khrushchev waved his hand dismissively: "It's totally out of place, totally out of place. You don't know anything. Listen to me: how many people are born in the Soviet Union every year?" "Three and half million" he is told. "Right, so until you, comrade Voznesensky, realize that you are nothing, you are one of these three and a half million, nothing will come of you. You are nothing! Put that up your nose."

Voznesensky was silent, or perhaps he mumbled something that I can't remember.

'After this screaming act of Khrushchev at Voznesensky a strange, cruel animation engulfed the crowd of intellectuals. Tolstoy in *War and Peace* has described this phenomenon well, when Rastopchin ordered the merchant's son to be killed and the whole crowd becomes infected with cruelty, and at first are indecisive but then get on with the killing.'

What did I mutter in answer to the head of state's 'You are nothing'? I bluntly repeated: 'I am a poet.'

V. Kaverin who was sitting near me, heard something else. In his article 'Solzhenitsyn' he said: 'Voznesensky was deathly pale, and he said: 'I am a student of Pasternak.'

From another stenograph my answers were recorded as: 'My contents are my poems.' 'Lies!' 'It's not lies!' 'Don't interrupt, let me finish what I'm saying. My work will show everything, there's no need for a speech.'

This is what Khrushchev said about Aksyonov and Golitsyn. 'Those two young men, when they applauded, they stuck their noses in. There they are the pair of them sitting there, one with glasses and one without.'

Other memoirs have appeared. This is how I looked from the side of the rostrum as an artist testifies: 'When the hall was roaring, and Khrushchev was crazed with anger behind his back, how horrible it was!' He remembers how Vasiliyevskaya, who was known to be close to Khrushchev, fell on my (that is Dostoyevsky's) banned saying 'Beauty will save the world'. It turned out that this phrase had undermined socialism in Poland. 'What sort of beauty?' she screamed. 'When it comes to Poland, it's a directive. This is harmful . . .' Prokofiev made a speech accusing me of not being a party member. 'I can't understand Voznesensky and so I protest. Such lack of ideology cannot and should not be borne by our literature.'

So my soul underwent an existential experience, at once common to my country and individual, which Berdyaev, the religious philosopher, maintains is formative for the character.

I've forgotten much, but my fingertips remember the icy Kremlin glass, rolling down the rostrum and they remember the sharp, crystal crosses of the facets on it. I wonder, if I had not stopped the glass, and it had fallen and smashed in front of the whole hall, perhaps Khrushchev would have come to from his fit, the atmosphere would have changed, cleaners would have come to sweep up the broken glass, the campaign would have been halted, there wouldn't have been any picking to pieces, or national scandal, and culture would have developed otherwise . . .

But the glass did not break. An accident of fate?

'The more accidental; the closer to reality.'

Heidegger: The Wisdom Tooth

His bony yellowish bald patch gleams. Martin Heidegger, the rooted tooth of German philosophy, is sitting, squat and strong, deep in a red armchair.

He is hidden in a dark corner of my memory, putting his roots in deep, sitting in the half-dark of a restaurant, measuring up to Wiener schnitzel. The last genius of European thought. The wisdom tooth.

It was his polished bald pate that I saw, although I could not make out the expression on his face, when I was performing at the Freiburg University. He sparkled on the right, rooted in his place, in a row of seats, even as a row of teeth, looking out suspiciously at the artificial smiles of progress radiating around. It was 14th of February 1967.

Then we had dinner which wouldn't have been worth mentioning, except for the fact that there flashed a crestfallenness, a thickset scowl, a hounded cautiousness about being with people. It was obvious that he had suffered greatly.

'Old Nazi', Inge said to me, when I told her about my visit.

The conversation took place at his home, in his study where the 'silent heavy tomes were like eight rows of teeth.' One of these rows was for the master's books. He was still alive and not put on the shelf. Martin Heidegger's cranium was still shining.

Our conversation was recorded by Count Podevils, the President of the Bavarian Academy. He had beetled down from Munich in his Volkswagen. He was refined, gaunt, with the French wind in his hair and he tipped me the wink that I had been elected to the Academy. He was erudite, had been a journalist in Paris for many years and revered his idol and was recording particular parts of our conversation. Unfortunately he recorded the master less than the guest, but even the words of the guest show what the great philosopher was interested in in 1967.

The Master actively led the conversation without holding back. This was another Heidegger, powerful but without arrogance, simultaneously helpless and wounded within, with a fractured soul.

'Quite quickly the conversation came round to the problem of the technical side which Voznesensky innovatively brings in to the language of his poetry. Voznesensky is an architect by training and is able to comprehend mathematical thinking but is alien to the sphere of technicalism, (here he is different from the avantgardists who only play with the scientific and technical lexicon).'

HEIDEGGER: Is the soul capable of being technical? Voznesensky mentions that within the audiences of many thousands there is a significant part that is from the young technical intelligentsia of Russia . . .

HEIDEGGER: 'Archi-techt! Techtonics. The meaning of the Greek word is "a senior builder". The architecture of poetry.' He even jumped up like a rooster as he cried out 'archi-techt.'

Often in his work the philosopher used the image of the church or temple on the cliff, as a metaphor for creation. Do you remember?

'The creation of the building in the church or temple does not reflect anything, but God is present in the temple through the temple. God is represented in the temple not so that it would be easier to acknowledge what He looks like; representation is creation, which allows God to be present, and is therefore divine. The same goes for creation in words. Creation allows the earth to be the earth.' Beauty is the means by which truth is in reality.

When I read these notes now of our conversation in Munich, which had been lying in the count's archive, I am struck by the congruity of ideas of the Freiburg Master with my own ideas even then when I had only heard of Heidegger (Heidegger's books, to our shame, are still not published in the Soviet Union). I read my words and they seem to be those of a completely different person. I was trying to read Heidegger in English then, but I seemed to be bashing my head up against the terms that were so difficult to translate. At that time we were engrossed in forbidden old volumes of Berdyaev, Kierkegaard and Shestov, who was writing articles about Husserl, from whose nest the Freiburg philosopher was hatched.

I knew of course that Sartre, whom I had been fated to meet, had emerged from Heidegger.

I look deep into my memory, and see not only his imposing forehead, but also his sharp lynx eyebrows, his bristly moustache, like a nail brush, his good three-piece suit, his animated eyes, which began to glimmer and sparkle like flames of brandy. I looked in them for a reflection of his love for his Marburg student, the young existentialist, the non-Arian, Hannah Arendt, and the tragedy of his split with her. But I couldn't penetrate through his face.

But I did ask him about Sartre.

He looked sullen, as though he was chewing the question over in his mind. Who was Sartre to him. Give him Chartres any day.

Sartre? The source of his originality lay in his poor knowledge of the German language. Sartre made a mistake and mistranslated two of the terms in my work. This mistake gave birth to his existentialism. There was almost a sensuality in the way the count took down this passage. The master sensed my disbelief and continued seriously:

'Voznesensky is asking how Heidegger feels about Sartre. Heidegger points out the difference. His own way of thinking is the making sense of "existence-here". Sartre is a representative of "existence". There is already a difference in language. The Heidegger understanding of "existence" is an ecstatic being: an openness to the present, past and future.'

'Voznesensky, picking up this idea, speaks about "the open poem" that counts on the active participation of the listener or reader.'

HEIDEGGER: The mutual connection with the poetical sphere.

VOZNESENSKY: A magnetic field.

Here the poem for Heidegger is just an ideal form of creation, the old idea: 'the creation of truth, which is implicit within the creation. The essence of poetry is such that art occupies an open position within existence, and in this opening all is unusual'. That is: 'openness within.'

The nervous face of Sartre, like a small broken mirror imposed itself on Heidegger's thick-set features. They were the same build. Their smoky faces devoid of their bodies, are fixed in my memory at the same level, like two glasses' lenses with separate prescriptions.

At that time the world was perplexed by the spiritual phenomenon of our poetry readings, whole stadiums of people listened to a single poet for hours on end. Both philosophers were interested in this phenomenon.

Sartre was at the reading and discussion of my book *Triangular Pear* in the Yelokhovsk library, in Moscow. He later wrote in an interview that this was the event that had most impressed him on his trip to Moscow. He stared like a madman at the rapt faces of the students. Sartre was with the monumental Simone de Beauvoir, and E. Zonina, who was the enigmatic 'Mme Z' to whom 'Words' is dedicated.

A school teacher criticized me from the floor for using words no one could understand like 'aqualung' 'transistor' 'poetaster' and for disrespect to the Generalissimo. The young audience laughed her out of court. Sartre leaned over and whispered to me: 'You must have hired her for this philippic.'

For several years I was enchanted by Sartre. I was interested at that time in existentialism. Sartre thirsted for sensations. He showed me 'Paris without clouds' in Paris, took me to 'Alkazar' where transsexual young men do striptease. He dragged me backstage in the interval where the young lads with fine busts were playing up to the guests. There was a smell of sweat as in a locker room. Simone's nostrils were quivering.

I took them to Kolomenskoye Church, where the architect had applied the principles of 'open and concealed beauty'. The great belfry is shielded by the silhouette of the gates till the very last moment, and its sudden appearance is a shock. The same technique is used in Japanese temples. Sartre wrote: 'I am often criticized as despising poetry: for instance they point to the fact that the journal *Temps Modernes* hardly publishes any poetry.' However, he refuted this by printing in *Temps Modernes* a selection of my poetry. He despised descriptive journalism in poetry: 'One shouldn't imagine that poets are involved with searching for the truth and explaining it. Poetry is something completely different. When a normal person is speaking he is the other side of the word, close to the object, and the poet is always on the other side. Since he does not know how to use the word as a symbol of this or another aspect of the world, he sees in it an image of one of these aspects.'

In my poem 'Paris Without Rhymes' this is how I described him:

> But Sartre, our dear Sartre,
> Is pensive as a gentle cricket . . .
> The cricket is silent on the leaf,
> And his face is crazy and tormented.

Ilya Ehrenburg was shocked: 'How could Sartre be a cricket? A cricket is light and graceful, but Sartre is more like a toad.'

'Have you ever seen the face of a cricket? Its face is an exact copy of the realistic face of Sartre,' I said in my defence. A week later, Ehrenburg, having seen the head of a cricket in a museum, said: 'You're absolutely right.' Ehrenburg sent me the following telegram, in that terrible New Year after Khrushchev had attacked the intelligentsia: 'I wish you a happy New Year of frolicking in the meadow with all the crickets of the world.'

But, alas, my contact with Sartre was broken off because of Pasternak. When he refused the Nobel Prize, Sartre accused the Swedish Academy of dealing in politics and also attacked Pasternak. This brought about wild rejoicing in the camp of our retrogrades, who up to then had branded Sartre.

Soon after, he invited me to a dinner which was being given in his honour in the Central House of Literature. I always find difficult the barbed stings and explanations of relationships. I called the guest away from the table and said: 'You don't understand our affairs. Why did you insult Pasternak?' And in order to cut off any avenue towards a reconciliation I added boldly: 'Everybody knows you refused the prize because of Camus.' Albert Camus had received the prize before Sartre and in his Nobel speech had enthused about Pasternak. This was rude, unjust and juvenile of me. I never met Sartre again.

But let's go back to the notes that were taken in Freiburg:

'The conversation turned to metaphor which, according to Heidegger, belongs to the sphere of poetry, the primal origin of language, where the word was open and many-sided. Mono-meaning is a narrowing which comes with science and logic.'

For me, metaphor has always been a technical means, and a connection between 'existence – here' and 'existence – there'. It is not a coincidence that Job expressed his most soul-searing idea as a metaphor: '. . . My screams were weighed . . . sands of the sea!'

Shestov, one of the fathers of existentialism's best book was born from this metaphor. I declared fierily in 1962: 'Metaphor is the motor of form.'

I tried to explain to Heidegger the rudiments of melo-metaphorism, which I was testing out at the time.

VOZNESENSKY: The written word is like a score, which comes to life in sound. It indicates that it belongs to the 'musical' movement in modern Russian poetry and this line comes from the old traditions, the bards, the singers (one could find a comparison in the Celtic tradition of Western Europe and Ireland). Alexander Blok and Mandelstam read their poems aloud stressing the rhythm before they were printed. Voznesensky feels that he belongs to this school. When he answered the accusation in Munich of being too declamatory, and that this was alien to the European tradition, Voznesensky pointed to this Russian tradition, and that his reading is a performance and creation of the poem as a creative act with the maximum inner concentration.

The thought came to me then, just what could a German philosopher understand of this unfamiliar semi-Asian Russian speech and construction, when he was listening with his bony forehead sparkling in the black gum of the front row of the student theatre?

As his academic circumstantial analysis proves, he saw in Russian poetics just a reinforcement of his own theses. He took 'I am Goya' as an expression of the primal language with its two 'ya's' at the end, which for him was the Greek 'beginning and ending', that is, the two single principles of creation ['ya' is 'I' in Russian. Tr]. It reminded me of a pencil sharpened at both ends and probably a red and blue pencil, but perhaps they have other sorts of pencils in Germany. I didn't always understand but I just nodded in agreement. Later, when I read his books, I heard his voice coming through the text, 'Language is not poetry because pre-poetry is in it, but it is poetry because it is present in the language and that language preserves the original essence of poetry . . . Truth directs itself into the heart of creation . . .'

I was sweating profusely on stage when I read in Freiburg. I very much wanted him to grasp the poems. My translator that night was Sasha Kempfe, a lovable rogue, the translator of Solzhenitsyn and the 'New Wave'. His shirt and trousers were garish and he puffed and blew and was in complete contrast to the prim and proper Count. When the Count talked Sasha was jealous and tugged at his handkerchief in his sweaty palm.

For Heidegger the visual metaphors of 'Oza' were closer, perhaps because this was more translatable and reminded him of the structure of the poetics of his youth and struck a chord within him of hatred of the technical revolution. It was a completely trans-parent object in his terminology.

The Count drily comments on the conversation. 'In his conversation with Heidegger, Voznesensky touched upon the problem of translation as he did in his introductory words to his reading at Freiburg University. Even the best translation is imperfect. But that also refers to poetry itself which translates things and is the "voice" of things in the sphere of the poetic word. But there is always something remaining of a secret, something ununderstandable (precisely because the translation does not operate on the single-language language of logic.) (Here, Heidegger nodded.) Nonetheless, people understand poetry especially when they listen to it, almost in the same way as the Latin and ancient Greek liturgies are understandable, even if they are being performed in an unfamiliar language. Heidegger asked about the meaning of the word truth. I answered that truth is in the creation.

VOZNESENSKY: Truth is not only truth but justice, correctness, an indicator of how to act and do things. The word '*istina*' (truth) comes from the root '*yest*'. ('There is' or 'there exists' Tr.) Here one has in mind action, existence, being. Poetry is involved with the revelation of truth.

I answered that the truth is in the creation.

HEIDEGGER. Poetry produces nothing, it shows. (Language is a 'showing'.)

Here we come to the main property of poetry according to Heidegger. He defined it with the word 'outlining' or 'sketching out', 'projection' of the future.

We read in Khlebnikov that 'There was a promise of finding the laws of time written on a silver birch (in the village of Burmakin in the Yaroslav province) foretelling the Tsushima disaster. There was also a brilliant prophesy of the revolution of 1917, made a few years before it.' It's doubtful that Khrushchev was an admirer of Khlebnikov but it's possible that the idea of the Sovnarkhoz that destroyed him (SNKH –Soviet Peoples' Collective Farms) came to him through his initials N.S.KH.

Poetry can not only sense the echo after an event, but also the echo preceding the event, which we can call the 'preecho'. The preecho, in the same way as animals feel an earthquake coming, preguesses the happening. In 'shadagam, magadam, pizz, pazz' he preguessed 'Magadam (a Siberian labour camp) the capital of the Kolyma region' and the ricochetting of bullets on icy stone.

There is an affirmation of a favourite thought of Berdyaev, that the body is not material, but the form of the soul.

In this sense the existentialism of the poetry of the sixties served well as the basis of many of today's spiritual processes. With its metaphorisms, rhythm, and search for a new structure of language, in opposition to the stereotypes of the System, poetry foresaw the chaos of today's processes, a chaos that is in search of constructivity. Poetry manifested itself as 'a personalized revolution, which really had not existed in the world, and meant an overthrow of the power of objectivity, and a breakthrough into another, spiritual world.'

Berdyaev says: 'Here the subject of philosophical knowledge is existential. In this sense my philosophy is more existential than Heidegger's philosophy.' Berdyaev frequently explains his relationship to Heidegger, acknowledging his talent, but noting his rationalism and the incomparability of their existential experience. I found a different Heidegger, who had suffered through his break-up with Hanna – alas, even geniuses become the slaves of family ties and slanders – and had survived her leaving Marburg to study first with Husserl and then Jaspers and then leaving Nazi Europe, having survived the collapse of illusions, the ostracism of the crowd, first the right, then the left, and his existential experience had spiritually broken him. Hanna called his thought 'passionate'.

Why did I go as a messenger to Heidegger?

In the floodwater of the sixties there was a desire for fundamental ontological truth. There was a year to go before the collapse of hopes in Paris, but there was already a sense of alarm. In the name of the last German genius the rare, for the Russian ear, sounds 'h' 'gg' 'r' rustled, which had so entranced the futurists in the first quarter of the century. Apart from this I was probably latently attracted by the parallel with Pasternak, my Peredelkino teacher, who studied philosophy under Cohen at Marburg. In the twenties Heidegger had occupied that chair at Marburg. I was also attracted by the thinker being an outcast, and his disgrace with the masses. Our meeting in Freiburg gave me much and reinforced much in me. The tempo of the trip did not allow me to stop and work out what I had heard. On top of Heidegger's words were the layers of conversations with M. Fried, with the 'new left', that were close to me, despite our violent arguments (many of whom were engrossed in Hanna Arendt), with V. Kazakov, who was criticized by our officialdom, with G. Yukker, who had made works of art from nails, which were the atipodes to the Russian works of wooden art, made without nails.

One should say that Munich, where the Academy was, was represented by our militant propaganda as a nest of vengeance, for Radio Liberty, which was jammed, was located there. However it was precisely the Munich Academy and Podevils himself who tried to make our cultures closer. It was at that time that the Academy had decided to select and invite writers from Russia. My selection was at almost the same time as the selection of A. I. Solzhenitsyn. Kempfe questioned me about Solzhenitsyn – it was as a result of his translating him that he was not allowed into Russia. He was interested in everything about the author of the Gulag. I told him all I knew. I had never got to know him closely. Yuri Lyubimov had introduced us in his room, when Solzhenitsyn had gone backstage after watching a performance of 'Antiworlds'. We talked and he said a few kind words about the show. Another time Z. Boguslavskaya and I had picked him up from Korney Chukovsky's dacha in Peredelkino. Chukovsky had asked us to give him a lift.

When we came out of the gates, the car got lodged in a rut. It was wet. We had to push the car out together. He was at the back on the left, and he got soaked in liquid mud from the damn wheels. His coat was completely drenched. We had to go back. Korney Chukovsky, groaning and gesticulating, let us wash ourselves down and then we continued without being properly dry. He didn't pay any attention to this. We talked for half an hour on the way. I wrote about this in the poem 'Foul Weather' (page 90), which I succeeded in printing in a book in 1975. Then A. Solzhenitsyn wrote me a note for the Central Archive Library, allowing me to read his novel *The First Circle*, which was then already confiscated. When I went to the States, I managed to visit M. Rostropovich, Ernst Neizvestny, and the poet N. Korzhavin and others I'd been close to in Moscow. I didn't get to see Solzhenitsyn; knowing how tight his schedule was I did not try to impinge on his solitude.

God is revealed within the creation, Heidegger teaches. Nowadays the name of the philosopher does not mean much to the public.

In Cologne a Heidegger Society has sprung up, but do we have a Berdyaev Society?

In June 1989 in the House of Literature, a miniature, little troll-like woman in doll's trousers stopped me. 'My name is Renata. I am a history professor in Freiburg. I saw you with Heidegger when I was a student. I must admit he wasn't really very interesting to us then. We came to see you.' A foreigner who had popped in was more interesting to them than the genius of their fatherland! He was accused of being blinded by the Reich. 'The lost genius'. H. Arendt.

Were Shostakovich, Pasternak and Korin, who lived and worked under the regime, to blame for Stalinism?

Hanna called him almost the murderer of Husserl in a letter to Jaspers. Hanna restrained him from getting too involved in the Italian futurists, since she considered them similar to *Mein Kampf*.

His character remained the same and, despite all effects of the environment, attracts young Americans.

In June I was witness to an African in a purple toga, fierily discussing Heidegger. This was in Budapest where the Getty Cultural Fund, founded by the contemporary Western Maecenases, Ann Getty, a beautiful woman with beautiful dreams, and Lord Weidenfeld, the publisher, who had published *Lolita* and fought it through the courts. They are moved by a mission to preserve truth.

It was a hot day. The wild forest of one part of the cemetery was roasting. We put roses, which had faded on the way, on the grave of Imre Nagy, among the pile of yesterday's wreaths and three-coloured ribbons. Imre Nagy and his comrades, after being murdered had been buried under assumed names, face down, so that their corpses could be further insulted. 'You want a Hungarian revolution?' I hear the old shout of Khrushchev in the Kremlin.

And a recorded transmission in the Palace Halls of the Academy was going on of an argument on European African and Asian culture. Within the essence of truth there is an argument for an open middle ground, to which one comes and from which all that exists comes.

West-truth? East-truth?

So, Africa was talking about Heidegger. The transcendental Durrenmatt wiped the lofty mist off his glasses, and declared that the nationalist wave only carried philosophy downstream and people tried to use philosophy in favour of ununderstandableness.

The Nobel Laureate and wonderful poet Czeslaw Milosz became involved in the conversation, as did the grey-bearded Robbe-Grillet and Adam Michnik, the favourite of the forum, the fawn of *Solidarity*, an inveterate reader of Russian literature, and the prose writer from South Africa, Nadine Gordimer, and Susan Sontag.

When I told of my meeting with Heidegger, it turned out that none of those there had ever talked with him. To tell the truth, it was strange that it was not a German but a Russian who read extracts of his conversation with the European philosopher. It was then that I decided to publish these pages, since it would be criminal to conceal anything however trivial that involved the genius.

In the count's notes there are further grains of unknown information. For instance Heidegger in his works does not once mention Sigmund Freud. This is despite the fact that they have much in common, and the students of Freud especially the Swiss, Binsvanger, openly combine Freud with Heidegger.

The count noted down:

'Voznesensky asks Heidegger's attitude to psychoanalysis. Heidegger declares himself to be against it. He decisively separates himself from Freud and his disciples.'

'Voznesensky tells how after the publication of the long poem "Oza" three psychoanalysts came to his house, to check up on his psychological state. They had noted psychological anomalies in certain fragments of the poem. However, fortunately for him the conclusions of all three were at odds with each other . . .'

The naive count! He thought that all our psychiatrists were psychoanalysts. Freud, alas, was banned then in Russia.

After the war Hanna sent him an unsigned card. 'I am here.' They met. He drily commented: 'Hanna had not changed at all in twenty-five years.' In her diary she called him 'the last great romantic'. But for many H. Arendt became closer as a philosopher than Heidegger. W. H. Auden was fond of her work. He told me that he wrote as though for her. He was prepared even to marry her.

I turn the last page of the transcript. The count, the pricked bubble of Sasha, the coat of the great enigmatic host, the earthen envelopes of ideas, all dissolve. They had vanished, leaving us with questions. Is it possible to make a draft of truth?

Are we here historically, in our here and now existence, at the source? Do we know the essence of the source, can we sense it? Or do we rely on our relationship to art on a studied knowledge of the past?'

How is our draft-existentialism of today? Can a genius be a fascist? Can art create a third reality? What does our monstrous existentialist experience give birth to in the form of revelation?

Will our descendants identify the skull of our epoch with the rooted tooth of the genius Heidegger?

PASTERNAK

The Annunciation of Objects by the Poet

Pasternak is the presence of God in our life. A presence as a fact, not postulated but objective. A sensitive feeling for life – the best inexplicable creation of the universe.

The rain is granted as the presence of God in him, the fir forest as the presence of God. God is given in details, swifts, raindrops, in cuff links, and our feeling is in the clear aspect of God before anything.

For the poet each object is an Annunciation. I'd like to talk about Pasternak's Annunciation. It is an exhibition, full of things that give tidings of God.

There are shells that sound and shells that are dead.

The poet's objects are sounding shells, which are always filled with something else apart from the shell.

Here is how he describes a shadow: 'It shined, as did the tea-glass holder.' Even in the darkness the poet sees the light. He himself went around in a single-breasted jacket with the suffused play of colours of copper and nickel. From him came a shining.

If this was only murmured in 'My Sister Life', at the end of the road it was told of clearly, like a sign.

> You meant everything in my fate.
> Then the war came and we were parted.
> And for such a long time
> I had not the tiniest bit of news of you.
> After many, many years
> your image woke me in alarm.
> All my life I read your testament
> and came to as though I had fainted.

I always felt that our meetings were with the reflected light of God present in him. He was the windows into the place of worship. This presence was maximized in the image of man or woman. I never met anyone like him. This was felt by both the élite and the ordinary workers in Peredelkino.

Nowadays looking at the sum of the century, in weighing up and measuring, we try to find an alternative to Stalin – Trotsky? Bukharin? Rykov? But these are all, alas, chesspieces on the same board. Pasternak has become the spiritual alternative to the tyrant. The Twentieth Century chose him for the solution of the well-known Russian juxtaposition: Poet and Tsar, Power and Spirit, incarnated in the solitary individual. The tyrant with his mystical superstition understood this and did not touch the poet. The poet tried to talk to the tyrant on the telephone about life and death, that is about God. The messianism of Pasternak, which he felt comes from this.

Even his initials 'B.P.' indicate that he was Beyond the Party (B.P. was the standard official formula for non-party people.)

At that time there were many great poets – Gumilyov, Akhmatova, Mandelstam, Yesenin, Mayakovsky, Zabolotsky, but time and what we understand by God, chose Pasternak himself. When Khrushchev assumed the throne, Pasternak became the spiritual alternative again. The Head of State, although cultural matters were not his forte, understood the hostility of the spiritual pole of power to the instinct of a politician and the quick grasp of an anti-intelligentsia man. Sitting in his box, he let loose Semichastny like a hunter to bark out what he had been taught in the stadium of the author of *Doctor Zhivago*. His anti-spirituality sensed danger.

No one ever put it more precisely than Pasternak himself, in a poem dedicated to Pilnyak:

> The poet's seat is wrongly left vacant
> in the days of the great Soviet,
> when the places of supreme passion are allocated.
> It is dangerous if it is not empty.

His Muse like Pushkin's is also polyphonic.

When an art critic asks us what comes to mind when one looks at the melting clock-face with the ants of Salvador Dali, one's memory brings up immediately:

> Clocks melted. Iridescent insects melted.
> The glass of the dragonflies scurried over cheeks.
> The forest was filled with hustle and bustle
> as though it was under the clockmaker's tweezers.

And here is Russian abstractionism:

> It is better to sleep, sleep, sleep
> and see no dreams . . .
> The soul is suffocating. And tobacco in the distance
> is like thoughts on snuff.

'Youth in the honeycomb' and 'The blossoming lilac' return us to the beehives of P. Filonov.

I should also mention the landscapes of his last years, with the Nesterov tear, with the Korin Northern frescoes, and of his great classic Christian canvasses, which go with the old masters of the Renaissance.

> Halls, halls, everywhere halls
> as though at an exhibition of paintings.

The poet started with a 'cup of chocolate' steaming in the mirror and 'We were the music of cups going off to have tea in the darkness', and he finished with the cup in the garden of Gethsemane.

> If it be only possible, Abba father,
> let this cup be carried past me.

It is symbolic that this cup of 'Hamlet' was not let into print in its entirety. As a result it became the final words from the lips of the dying poet.

The interaction between Pasternak and his contemporaries is huge. He defined much not only in poetry but also in the prose of this century. Even Vladimir Nabokov, who envied his Nobel prize, who accused him of Benedictinism etc., as a poet was not free to the end of his days from the influence of Pasternak. And how about in prose?

Let's remember Nabokov's great book *Luzhin's Defence*. You remember how the hero, the Russian chess genius, goes out on to the moonlit terrace of the small German town. He remembers his rival Turati. The night is filled with black and white figures. The trees are figures. The moonlight makes the terrace like a chess board. His loved one sits on his lap. He makes her get off. She witnesses his suffering. The night, with its black and white figures is a chess match. Where have we read this? A Russian would look at the Marburg night in Pasternak's poem.

You see, the nights sit down to play chess
with me on the moonlit parquet floor.
The windows are wide open and you can smell the acacias,
and passion grows grey in the corner and witnesses it all.

The poplar is the king. And I am playing sleeplessness.
The queen is the nightingale, and I am drawn to the nightingale.
Night is winning, the pieces are scattered.

'Marburg' is the ovary of Nabokov's novel.

Our's is a special exhibition. This exhibition is a novel in space. To wander round it is like going through the halls and rooms of *Doctor Zhivago*, leading to the spiritual finale, the altar. *Doctor Zhivago* is a special type of novel, it is a poetic novel. It is also about God's presence in us and of our abandonment of him.

The huge corpus of prose is like an overgrown lilac bush, bearing double clusters of poems that crown it. Since the aim of the bush is the clusters of flowers, or in the case of the apple tree – apples, so the aim of the novel is the poems which grow out of it in the finale. We see how in the process of life, in the troubled soul of the author and the hero of the novel, the flame of the candle glimmers at the beginning, seen through the frosty window, and in this light appears 'Blok, who is the manifestation of Christmas in Russian life', then the sensitive candle at night becomes the symbol of his love for Lara, the snowstorm, the symbol of history, blows out the solitary candle stump, and personalities, spiritualization and the intelligentsia perish – and finally in the finale of the novel the miracle of the classical poem blossoms: 'The candle burned on the table', without whose light it is impossible to represent our spiritual culture. There also the light of the 'Christmas Star' arises from the fate of the hero, and Hamlet's groan: 'I am alone, all drowns in Pharisaism/Living one's life through is not a walk across a field.'

Pasternak's prose is in no way an article on 'How to Write Poetry', no it is a novel, the life of a poet, a novel about how to live by poetry, and how poems are born in life. There has never been a novel like that.

The works of the Classics obstinately live in time. Their sense is like a flower which opens to the reader, but then can be closed to him. Thus it is with Turgenev's novels, and Joyce's.

But alas, *Doctor Zhivago* is now not simply a book – it is a novel overlaid with shameful events. Our thirty years of propaganda, without it even having been read, and not becoming engrossed in the lyrical music of its magic Russian language, made out the novel to be a political monster and a libel. And now the novel is printed, and printed in a series of hot, contemporary, great social works. I think that quite a few of the millions of readers, who subscribed to 'Novy Mir' for the publication of *Doctor Zhivago* would find themselves in disbelief at the monstrous lies of thirty years surrounding the novel and its lyrical pages! Why did they persecute the author? Why did they exclude him from the Union of Writers? Why did they prepare to have him exiled? For the love passages on Yuri and Lara? For the fevered description of the nightingale trill, which can be compared with those of Turgenev. Apart from the crimes against the poet as an individual, there was a long standing crime against the sense of the novel. As a result of the abuse against the novel throughout the Soviet Union it is impossible now to read it objectively. In vain now do readers search for the promised seditious element. Eardrums, that are expecting a cannonade, cannot appreciate the music of Brahms.

The guilt of disinformation lies with those who carried out the literary intrigues of those days, and they were led by A. Surkov. Provoked by them N. S. Khrushchev organized the persecution of Pasternak with the same temperament and broad sweep as in the Caribbean epic, or the quest in space or in agriculture for sweetcorn.

Semichastny rapturously shouted out the governmental metaphor: 'If you compare Pasternak to a pig, then the pig wouldn't have done what Pasternak has. He has shitted in his own trough . . .' Then without a shadow of recantation the retired orator opened up the level of piggishness in which this pig had been born: 'I remember we were invited to Khrushchev in the Kremlin on the eve of the Plenary Meeting. That was me and Adzhubey and Suslov was there too. He said, 'We must work over Pasternak in the statement. Let's discuss it now and you can edit it later. Suslov will look it over and tomorrow . . .' He dictated two pages. Of course this was from the abrupt position of where 'even a pig doesn't shit in . . .' There was this phrase also: 'I think that the Soviet Government would not be against Pasternak's leaving our homeland if he so wants to breathe in the air of freedom.' 'You say it and we'll applaud. They'll take it up.' Thus in agreement with the highest authority the orchestrated process was transmitted on television across the whole country. Immediately after the bit about where the pig doesn't shit they showed the threatening applause of Khrushchev and his comrades-in-arms. The poet had forecast this.

Every day is so blunt before one
that reality is hard to bear:
the photographed groups
with ugly faces just like pigs.

Here are a few quotations from the shameful witches' sabbath of the meeting of writers of 27 October 1958, which excluded the poet and demanded that the government send him into exile. The speakers attempted to remain close to the Head of the Government. The transcription, which has now been published, became a political document about the most apolitical poet. 'Pasternak is really a literary Vlasov. The Soviet court gave the order for Vlasov to be shot. (Shouts of 'He was hung.') Out of this country, Mr Pasternak. We don't want to breathe the same air as you!'

The venerable critic announced: 'Let him leave the country. It's hard for me and our comrades to believe that such people live in our writers' village. I cannot imagine now having Pasternak as a neighbour. He shouldn't be even in the census of the population of the USSR.'

This is about Pasternak, the best poet of our times, to breathe the air of whose poems was a rare happiness, as it was to breathe the crystal air of Lake Baikal and the Aral sea, whose miracle has also been blindly destroyed!

It is completely logical that this critic preparing the way for the meeting on Pasternak, should write on 9th September 1958 in the *Literary Gazette*, 'The religious epigonic poems of Pasternak smell of moth balls from the symbolists' chest of 1908–1910.'

And here is a letter from a well-known writer to the sixty-eight-year-old poet. '. . . Traitors should be shot in the back of the neck. I am a woman who has seen much grief. I am not an evil woman, but facing this treachery I wouldn't flinch to . . .'

What it must have been like for Pasternak to read this? But let's learn from the magnanimity of the patriarch of poetry. He answered this 'kind, lady-Zhdanov in a skirt'; '1st November 1958. Thank you for your frankness. The years of the Stalin terror, which I had seen in their true light before they were unmasked, altered me . . . You are younger than me and will live to a time when the past will be looked at in another light. I am writing to you so that you would realize that I didn't hold back from answering you. B. Pasternak.'

It's a pity that the writer of the letter did not live to see these days. But it is an even greater shame that Pasternak did not.

On 1st November 1958, the *Literary Gazette* wrote: 'It is not by chance that Bukharin wrote him a panegyric!' 'Is not *Doctor Zhivago* the spiritual son of Klim Samgin. Gorky unmasked Samgin. Pasternak in *Zhivago* unmasked himself.' The hero is the author, so he had to be exiled!

Today, on the eve of the centenary of the author, the political opponents of the renewal of the country are in rage about the novel, whose author they call a newly appeared genius, as one almost illiterate thinker expressed himself. They reprint the slanders from the persecution times in the main newspapers, even in a column in *Pravda*, and about Klim Samgin and that the poems from the novel repeat the 'divergent poetry of that time'. As an example one of the critics quotes 'White Night', one of the pearls of Russian lyric poetry.

> The street lamps are like butterflies of gas.
> The morning shuddered into being.
> What I tell you quietly
> is so like the sleeping distances.
> We are seized by the same
> timid faithfulness to the secret,
> like Petersburg is to the stretched panorama
> over the boundless Neva.

Praise the Lord if just one more such poem could delight Russian poetry! Apparently the critic is unlucky enough not to understand this music, the music of poetry, the music of conscience which makes the content of the novel. My answer to this article was printed in *Pravda* along with an alternative opinion – the advantages of pluralism face to face. At the same time, incidentally, the phrases of the stenographed process on Pasternak were printed for mass circulation.

I don't bring this critic in as an example because of his significance, but simply as an example of what even now is ignoble in the Pasternak affair. As for the rantings of *Molodaya Gvardiya* (Young Guard) they searched for the evidence of the Pharisee, 'fawning before them like a fox.' These are truly prophetic lines.

His lines are compressed in the poems, like the muscle of the heart.

How achingly the lines are cut in 'Winter Night'! Pasternak loved to work with the shortened line.

> In everything I want to get to
> the essence.

Most poets would have gone rolling on on the iambic track:

> In everything I want to get to
> the most treasured essence . . .

But the master cuts back and compresses the even line, visually pointing out the 'compression' of the essence . . .
In the poem 'Winter Night' the aim is different:

> The candle burned on the table,
> the candle burned.

Here the sensation is captured physically of the long candle burning down like the poem till it is a stump. Then a new candle is put in and it burns. Candle, passion, life.
It's not for nothing that A. Galich for his song dedicated to Pasternak's trials chose precisely this angry measure, that squeezes and unsqueezes with alarm.

> We will remember everyone by name
> who lifted their hands . . .

But let's return to the judges of the novel now.
'Much can be forgiven if the writer is intelligent and talented' and the newspaper critic writes condescendingly, musing about the author of the poems in the novel: 'Is he intelligent or not? Is he talented or untalented?' But the measure of the talent is not in the administrative posts the author has, or in a nomenclatural editorial chair, no, the measure of talent is in poetry alone. And the poems in the novel are great poems in the Russian classical tradition: 'Fable', 'Summer in the City', 'Parting', 'Magdalen'.
The critic berates the post, the author of the poems, with 'mediocrity', 'a successful bureaucrat all the way to grey hairs,' a second-class poet or a mediocre translator'. These arrows, alas, are not fired at the hero of the novel. The novel is written in a method of metaphorical autobiography. All the heroes and events have their prototypes in Pasternak's life. In Nikolai Nikolaevich we see Bely and Skryabin, Strelnikov is the spiritual metaphor of Mayakovsky. Urnov, the writer of the article and a doctor of philology knows that Pasternak wrote: 'This hero represents something between me, Blok, Yesenin and Mayakovsky. And when I write poems now I write them into the "Yuri Zhivago notebook". So the criticism of "mediocrity"

is consciously aimed against Pasternak, the deepest poet of our century! And a citizen.'

In 1937 when signatures to a letter were being collected approving the death sentence on Yakir, Tukhachevsky and others, Pasternak was the only writer who refused to sign this shameful letter. In the novel we read a passage that shows a risk in real life: 'The vast majority of us are constantly demanded under the system to display a warped mentality.'

Critics shyly call the persecution of a poet 'a misfortune'. Why can't we call things by their real names?

'The poems are no better, no deeper, than the philosophy in the novel itself,' the critic writes carefreely. The fact that these poems are great is known even to schoolchildren. If we take at random some of the 'philosophy' from the novel. 'The main trouble and the root of future evil was the loss of belief in personal opinions. The tyranny of the phrase began to grow.' This was written forty years ago and is not without depth.

'Although enlightenment and liberation which were expected after the war did not come with victory, as people had thought they would, nevertheless the portent of freedom was carried on the air throughout those after-war years, leaving their unique, historical content.' This too is not without depth and these lines seem to be aimed at the present times.

His reasonings on Christianity are deep too and without them one cannot grasp the thousand-year history of our homeland, and behind them stand the depths of spiritual history: the icon-painter Dionysus, the church of Pokrov-na-Nerli, Tolstoy, Dostoyevsky, the religious philosopher Florensky, the philosopher-historian Vernadsky.

The New Testament theme is resolved amazingly enough in Russian – with frost, wolves and dark fir forests.

The poet understands Christ as a new phenomenon, a turn in history's path, when 'man dies not under the fence by the street, but almost at home in history, burning full of work which is dedicated to the overcoming of death. If it was possible to stop the beast dozing within humanity with a threat, whatever confinements or recompense beyond the grave exist, the emblem of humanity would still be the circus tamer with his whip and not the preacher who sacrifices himself. But the thing is that it was not the stick that lifted humanity up, but music: the inexpressibility of unarmed truth . . .'

For the poet, Christianity is humanity and spirituality. Nowadays, when there is a publicistic unmasking of Stalin which is at times primitive, at times as a state of the nation, it is important at times to remember Pasternak's philosophical interpretation of him as an executioner. Once in conversation he referred to Stalin as a despot of the 'pre-Christian era' like Herod, or 'Caligula with his pock marks.'

The theme of Christianity in prose and poetry does not appear by chance.

The novel is hard to read. It is an anti-bestseller really, but in world literature there are few pages as powerful cinematographically as, say, the description of the death of the hero, who chokes to death in a tram that's pulling away slowly. It catches up or hangs behind the figure of a woman – life, death, or fate.

The enemies of the novel try to prop up their ununderstanding of the novel by referring to their second rate western colleagues. For me Albert Camus' evaluation of the novel is the most authoritative.

At the decision of UNESCO, 1990 has been designated the 100th jubilee year of Boris Pasternak. I cannot say that the return of justice to the poet in our country has occurred or passed without difficulties. The fight for the museum alone was like beating one's head against a rubber wall. N. A. Pasternak, who is the present head of the Peredelkino memorial of the poet, who has been preserving his things, found a file in his desk. On it is written in Pasternak's hand 'Andryusha's poems'. My fate is only interesting here as an example of his caring for others. It turned out that he had kept in this file over the years my boyish letters, with their envelopes even, and their naive poems – and in their margins he had underlined what he liked. What he didn't like he had crossed out faintly in pencil. It is only now that I realize how attentive he was.

Thanks to the initiative of the commission on the heritage of Boris Pasternak the shameful decision to remove the poet from the Union of Writers has been rescinded. To restore him to the Union of Writers would be blasphemous. However some superficial journalists continue to demand emphatically his restoration as a member of the Writers' Union. Should he be given his membership card in the grave? Should he be congratulated on his coming back? He was mocked enough during his lifetime. The Pasternak commission was the first to act; Pasternak always fought for others. In the wake of the Pasternak commission the shameful decisions to remove from the Union of Writers O. Mandelstam, P. Vasiliev, I. Babel, V. Nekrasov, V. Meyerhold, M. Rostropovich, E. Etkind and others, were rescinded.

In the case of the living, of course they could be restored into the Unions, as for instance in the case of E. Etkind, as deep researcher into literature. Now the Union of Writers has its department in Paris – of one person, but E. Etkind is worth dozens of others. The second living rumour is that when Boris Pasternak was forced to refuse the prize he did not become the Nobel Laureate. Our commission sent a letter to the Swedish Academy with the idea of giving the medal to the family of the poet. I was in Stockholm and talked to the secretary of the Academy, Professor Allen, who was informally involved in the 'Pasternak Affair'. The question was referred to the next session. What a joy it was, although a late and bitter one, that in December the medal was presented in Stockholm to the son of the poet E. B. Pasternak.

All this: the fate of the poet, his century, of whom he became the double, surrounds us at the exhibition. We should thank the museum workers who created it. Let us walk through the halls of the genius of poetry who lived through and expressed the most terrifying century of humanity. Perhaps the manifestation of the poet is hope that humanity is not so hopeless after all.

When I visited Jerusalem, I was shocked at how true the landscapes are in the New Testament cycle in *Doctor Zhivago*: the road to Bethane, the road round the Mount of Olives, the water meadows of the Kedron, although the poet had in reality never been there. The hidden camera of the poet documentarily 'visits other worlds'. The clarity of vision of the poet cannot yet be explained by science.

Let us try to understand the Annunciation of Objects of the poet.

Instead of an Afterword

When this book is published, I don't know what will be happening to my country. Will it still be there? Will it have collapsed? Our country recorded championship feats in the XX century – the Gulag, Chernobyl. Thank the Lord that the Political System has collapsed and will perish. That's how it should be!

But it is paradoxical that my country simultaneously with totalitarianism gave wings to poetry in the XXth century: Akhmatova, Khlebnikov, Mandelstam, and readings of poems in stadiums. This year a book of Pasternak's poetry in a one million print run was sold out instantaneously. Throughout the country, confirming the thesis of Jacques Derrida of decentralization, young groups of poets are springing up. In Siberia, one of the best is called 'The Politburo'. It would be terrible, if with the collapse of the Political System the last country in the world should perish where millions read by heart poems as prayers; the country of Dostoyevsky, Pasternak. Will poetry, its one characteristic that distinguishes it, disappear? I wrote some lines in 1970 that became a popular song:

> Don't vanish. Even if we are on the edge.
> It doesn't matter if I vanish
> I won't let you.
> Don't vanish.

These lines were written to a woman. Now they are addressed to my spiritual land.

Notes

6   'First Love'
In the first verse is described the Russian method of making a Bloody Mary.

9   'Up the Lighthouse in Lithuania'
Written in the frontier town of Lithuania, Nida.

10 'Two-headed eagle'
This is printed in the underground Anthology *Metropol*. Since the two-headed eagle was the imperial symbol his critics accused Voznesensky of anti-Sovietism.

11 'Ballad of the Last Days in the Ipatyev House'
The Emperor Nikolai II's family was shot in the cellar of the Ipatyev house in Yekaterinburg in Siberia. Their bodies were dissolved in hydrochloric acid. The house was destroyed. Before it was destroyed Voznesensky visited it and stole a bit of the window through which they looked while they were being shot. He has preserved this object of Russian *art nouveau*.

14 'Lithuanian Motifs'
Justinas Martsinkyavichus is a Lithuanian poet. Voznesensky was the only Russian who spoke at the Soyudis (Lithuanian Popular Front) in 1988. This poem was read by a Lithuanian actress at the congress in the stadium. On 13 January 1991 Vozesensky sent a telegram to Gorbachov asking that the bloodshed in Lithuania stop. The secret protocols are the agreement between Stalin and Hitler.

15 'Curfew Time'
Written in Abkhasia. Kalashnikov is not only a machine gun but also a successful merchant in a Lermontov ballad.

17 'A. MEN'
The priest Alexander Men, who was Jewish born, was the universally respected spiritual leader of the Russian intelligentsia. He was murdered most probably by the right, from which he got death threats and anti-Semitic letters. Voznesensky was at the same school with him. In the novel *Brothers Karamazov* in the dialogue of Ivan Karamazov with the devil there is the idea of launching an axe as a sputnik.

19 'Chagall's Cornflowers'
Vitebsk is the birthplace of Chagall. Chagall illustrated Voznesensky's poem 'Ghetto in the Lake'. In 1973 Chagall came to visit Voznesensky's house in Peredelkino outside Moscow. This poem was attacked in the Soviet press as Zionist, since Chagall was accused of being a Zionist émigré and a modernist.

Voznesensky did much for the first exhibition of Chagall and the museum in Vitebsk. 'Voznesensky was the initiator of a hysterical campaign around the centenary of Chagall, who had lived abroad since 1922 and was connected with Byelorussia only by the fact of his having been born there.' Vecherny Minsk 22 June 1987.

23 'Videopoem'

'Communism is the Soviet Power + Electrification of the whole country': a favourite slogan of Lenin. Lenin V. I.: 1879–1924, the founder of the Soviet State.

25 'Applefall'

The poem was written in Picasso's house when Voznesensky was visiting his widow with his San Dominican friend in 1981. He remembers his meeting with Picasso in 1963. The cuts in the Russian texts for translation in 'Applefall' as elsewhere were made by Voznesensky, working with the translator.

42 'Crosses'

Kerensky, Alexander (1881–1971): Head of the Provisional Government in 1917. He attended a reading of Andrei Voznesensky in 1965 at Columbia University and talked with him.

65 'After the Tone'

Voznesensky gets many threatening phone calls and menacing letters from *Pamyat*. *Vertep* is one of the underground poetry groups that Voznesensky supports.

76 'Sergei Yesenin and Marina Tsvetayeva'

These great Russian poets both committed suicide by hanging.

78 'Black and White'

This was written in the Rasputin Bar in Paris.

81 'The Law of the Dragonfly'

In Russian *Aksiomasamoiska* (The Law of Self-seek-self) is a palin-drome and the title of Andrei Voznesensky's last book (1990) from which these poems come. 300,000 copies were printed, priced at 6 roubles. But at a charity auction it was sold (unsigned) for 120 roubles. Dziga Vetrov is the founder of the avant-garde documentary cinema in Russia.

86 'Her Story'

'Whore' in Russian is *'blyad'*. The author's usage of the word *'blyad'* caused righteous outrage at the Congress of Russian Writers and in the right-wing press in 1990.

87 'N. N. Berberova'

Nina Berberova, Russian émigré writer, former wife of the poet V. Khodasevich, author of the novel *The Iron Lady* which is now published in the USSR, with a foreword by Andrei Voznesensky. In Russia, unlike in Britain where traditionally 'accompanying gentlemen' walk on the traffic side of their ladies, it is usual to walk on the left side. However Russian officers would walk on the right side so that they could salute. Nikolai Gumilyov, poet and traveller, leader of the Acmeist movement, was shot in 1921, accused of participation in a counter-revolutionary plot, and only republished in Russia, after sixty years, under glasnost.

88 'Requiem for Vysotsky'
The poem was written in 1971 during the clinical death of Vladimir Vysotsky, a singer, poet and actor, the idol of Russia. Vladimir Semyonovich Vysotsky was the leading actor at the Taganka Theatre. The first play staged at the Taganka was Voznesensky's 'Antiworlds' in which Vysotsky played eighty times. Vladimir Vysotsky was the main actor in Voznesensky's second play; 'Save your Faces'. The play was closed down after two performances. The poem 'Requiem for Vysotsky' was printed in the magazine *Druzhba Narodov* under the title: 'Requiem to Vladimir Semyonov: a Driver and Guitarist'. This was the only poem to Vysotsky printed during his lifetime.

90 'Foul Weather'
See 'The Wisdom Tooth' p. 146. This poem was published in book form in 1975.

92 'Unauthorized Meeting'
These two poems were written after Voznesensky spoke on the same podium as Sakharov at a forbidden meeting as a protest at the murdering by tanks of Georgians in Tbilisi.

93 'Demonstration'
In Simonov's Memoirs he records that Stalin said: 'Foreigners are shits.'

94 'Proposal for a Memorial'
The approximate figure for those who died in the camps is 30,000,000. Titsian Tabidze was a Georgian poet and victim of Stalin. Berggolts, see Note to page 95.

95 'The Madonna of 1937'
Olga Fyodorovna Berggolts, a poet who was in the Gulag, wife of the poet Boris Kornilov, who was killed in the Gulag.

97 'The prisoners make the seat-covers for Aeroflot'
It is a fact not fiction that the cloth for the Aeroflot seats is made by Soviet convicts.

100 'A Cut-Diamond Fable'
The Order of Victory was made at Stalin's orders. Later a cheap variant was made and the expensive one was put in the museum. According to Soviet law Diamond orders have to be returned after the holder's death. As the story goes, Brezhnev granted himself the Order, and gave himself the diamond one from the museum. After his death the Order was returned but the diamonds had been extracted. His son-in-law was a general in the police.

102 'Belka and Strelka'
The names of the first Soviet dogs in space. Written in 1958 as a memorial to the dogs, Voznesensky read this poem in Boris Pasternak's house. First printed in 1990.

109 'Ditch' 'Introduction'
Just before 22 June 1941 Soviet archaeologists opened Tamerlane's tomb. The local old men had warned them that there was a myth that if the tomb was touched there would be a great war. On 22 July 1941 the war with Hitler began. Luzhniki is a stadium in Moscow where poetry readings were held.

117 'Debt'

The Arbat in Moscow was burned down by Napoleon in 1812. The Tartar yoke, or occupation of Russia lasted 300 years. The Arrow Express is the night train from Moscow to Leningrad.

118 'Farewell to the Microphone'

From 30 November 1962 Russian poets started reading in stadiums of 14,000 people. Voznesensky was one of the leading figures in this movement. It was the only place where the censor did not check their texts. Voznesensky has now gone over to a more visual approach to poetry.

120 'The Liturgy of Years'

'Lord have mercy' is the motif of Voznesensky's Rock Opera 'Juno and Avos'. Nagorno Karabakh is an Armenian enclave in Azerbaidzhan, for years the centre of bloody incidents. Yakov was Stalin's son, who died in captivity with the Germans. Stalin did not try to exchange him.

122 'Have you prayed tonight'

This is a line from *Othello*, Act V. Scene 2.

123 'The mount of decision' and 'Olive Branch'

These last two poems were written in Jerusalem in October 1989.

153 Pasternak

Suslov: the main ideologist of the Party. A. A. Surkov: secretary of the Writers' Union. Organizer of the persecution of Pasternak.

Andrei Voznesensky has written the introduction to a bilingual Centenary Anthology of Boris Pasternak, Osip Mandelstam and Anna Akhmatova to be co-published by *Ogonyok* in 1992, which includes new translations of all three poets by Richard and Elizabeth McKane, as well as some of their Akhmatova and Mandelstam that have appeared in the United Kingdom from Bloodaxe Books.